BOLD

LIVING INTENTIONALLY

IN TODAY'S WORLD

NICKI CORINNE WHITE

BOLD
LIVING INTENTIONALLY
IN TODAY'S WORLD

c 2021 by Nicki Corinne White

Published by Carpenter's Son Publishing, Franklin, Tennessee

All scripture quoted is NASB unless otherwise noted.
Copyright © 1960, 1962, 1963,
1968, 1971, 1972, 1973, 1975, 1977
1995 by The Lockman Foundation
Used by permission. (www.Lockman.org).

The MacArthur Study Bible. J. F. MacArthur Jr,
gen. ed. Nashville: Word, 1997.

Edited by David Brown
Cover illustration by Nicki Corinne White
Cover design by Jessica Owinyo
Back cover photo by Jamie Hudson
Interior design by Debbie Manning Sheppard
Printed in the United States of America
978-1-952025-7-92

ENDORSEMENTS

I clapped my hands and smiled many times as I read this book. The world is so desperate for hope, and we get to be hope-bringers to the world, but we must not hold our lives back to do so. Reading the stories of ordinary believers living their faith in bold, extraordinary ways empowered me to want to live in obedient boldness.

I loved the reminders in this book to live a bold life for Christ in the power of Christ. Full of stories of those living their brave yes to Jesus in different ways, this book encourages us to live our bold yes to Jesus, where He has called us.

Each story reminds us to live for God's glory in our own stories. The state of the world today is a key time for Christians to rise for such a time as this. This is a beautiful book to encourage us to live intentional lives.

JENNIFER HAND
Author of *My Yes is On the Table: Moving from Fear to Faith*
podcaster (*Comng Alive Conversations*),
and Executive Director of *Coming Alive Ministries*

Nicki is giving us each the opportunity for vicarious learning. What could be better! Real life God stories, presented to us in the gentlest way how trusting God works. And...trusting Him is absolutely fundamental.

Thank you Nicki!

LORETTA CHALFANT,

"These inspiring stories remind us of the cost, the joy, and the impact a bold follower of Christ can have. May the brave and intentional choices within these pages kindle a fiery love in your heart for following Jesus. This book will encourage you to stand for Him in a world full of hearts hungry for a beautiful gospel."

STACY AND HOLLY GORTON,
CRU Ministries

"Nicki White has grappled with what it means to be bold in our service and witness for the Lord, using both modern-day examples that resonate with us all and ancient biblical examples that have been familiar to us since our mother's knee. You will find her words helpful in applying Scripture to your own situation. Our times increasingly call for a greater boldness in our witness to the truths of God's Word in a world that is careening toward destruction."

PASTOR RANDY COOK
Meridian First Baptist Church

"We found the stories in BOLD to be challenging testimonies of modern day servants of the LORD. The theme of boldness comes through clearly as the selfless attitude of the individuals challenges the reader to reach out beyond one's comfort zone to share God's love with hurting people."

PASTOR TIM AND DONNA WELLS
CHURCH PLANTERS
PASTOR OF COLUMBIA HEIGHTS BAPTIST CHURCH

DEDICATION

To Pastor Darrell & Ruthanne
and to all the missionaries
sharing Christ around the world

I waited a while to decide who to write this dedication to because I kept thinking I should write it to one person. Then I started thinking about what the core message in this book was and then I knew it wasn't just one person but several. I became a believer as a young teen. I was going through a lot in my home life and just threw myself into youth group. I wanted to plan activities. I called through a list of kids every week to invite them. In my head I thought, "why don't they all want to come?" I lived for the interaction I got at church. It was everything to me. As a young believer I wanted to learn the Word, and memorized as much Scripture as I could. I went to every youth event and even got a chance to go to camp a couple times. And then a missionary came to our church and I decided I would be a missionary.

A big part of this growth was because of our pastor and wife. I went to a small country church and we didn't have a youth pastor. We had one pastor. He and his wife were young and had two little boys at the time. I have mentioned Pastor Darrell and Ruthanne in my two previous books for they encouraged my spiritual growth and were an integral part in my early Christian life. I wanted to learn everything I could. My home life seemed to be crumbling around me but church was the one thing I lived for.

Then I went to a small Christian college. There were kids from all over the states and other countries. Many of them had grown up in Christian homes. They loved me just the way I was and often gave me Bible verses that spurred me on to grow and encouraged my heart. There are too many to list but I would encourage you to make friends with people who will cause you to grow and not pull you under.

Then as I got married and was involved in a couple other churches I realized I loved when missionaries came to church or when there were missions conferences. And this is one thing that spurred me on to write this book. Each of these people were stepping out from the comfort of their home or town, they had to earn money to be able to go, they had to spend months preparing, and some of them have gone to very dangerous places in order to share the news of salvation in Jesus. They did this with great intention and purpose. Knowing that they will not have riches here on earth but that their reward is for eternity. They learned languages, sometimes many, to be able to go to the country they are serving in or maybe they are reaching out to people in the US and are serving those all around them.

Whatever the case, they are my heroes. They are the ones who encourage me to be bold in my faith. They are the ones who daily show me why we need to be bold, and help me to have that sense of urgency. Eternity is a long time. I had a friend in college who told me to put a sign on the refrigerator or mirror that reads, "Does it count for eternity?" What am I doing daily to show others the gospel of Christ?

I hope this book inspires you to be *BOLD* in your faith.

ACKNOWLEDGEMENTS

Jessica Everett and Maureen Loeffler - The two of you have worked many hours editing, inputting ideas, and helping plan this book. You are amazing, and this project would not have come to fruition without your help.

Craig White - Well Honey, so glad I have my own personal tech support at home, especially this year with having to zoom our team meetings. And your patience every time I said, "It's not working!"

Nathan White - We cannot have any sort of ministry without our websites. I really appreciate all your work in writing code for all our crazy additions and changes.

Jessica Owinyo - Moving to another state did not stop me from asking your wise advice on our creative needs with the team. You are always there to help. And the front cover looks great! SO thankful you put up with me!

Ashley Taylor, Karen Law, and Marsha Philbrook - Thank you Ashley for taking leadership in leading the Colossians 3:12 Ministries team this year and finding countless more resources to add. And Karen and Marsha, even though you are new to our team, it is great to have your help on this.

Jamie Hudson- Once again, we have your beautiful photos on the back cover and inside the book. Thank you so much for your vision and beautiful photography.

Tori Loeffler- Great to have you give your expertise in helping with these epigraphs.

Julie Taddicken- You have a talent for doing extra little details. Thank you for helping with some media posts when I was swamped.

Beta readers and pre-edits: Ruthanne, Julie, Jessica, and Re - I am constantly blessed by all of you. You help me when my mind is totally blocked. I could never get anything off to print without you!

MY AMAZING
CONTRIBUTORS

Dear Reader,

This book that you hold in your hand would not be possible without you. Without readers, there is nothing to say, and it is you and your journey that makes a book come to life. When we read something new, our minds expand with the possibility each sentence and paragraph holds. We choose to take it all in, learn, grow, and sometimes even apply those thoughts and words to our lives, enriching others. In doing so, you are my biggest contributor.

This is my third book. Each of my books has contained wonderful testimonies from people who encourage others through their own lives. This book also has testimonies woven throughout. Every one of these people were chosen because they have taken steps to go beyond the norm, to exceed expectations, and to live boldly. They are living life with purpose and intention. They do not back away when something gets tough. They live boldly, knowing God wants us to share His love with the world.

Because of some of the situations shared, we decided not to print full names, and some names have been changed for safety reasons. But the point of each testimony is not the who, but the why and how these people ministered to others. I pray as you draw in their stories, that your heart is enriched by them. We are all con-

nected by feelings, experiences, and emotions, each one a part of the bigger picture of God's perfect plan.

I cannot tell you how grateful I am to each of these people for sharing part of their story in this book so it may encourage you in your own walk to boldness.

"Be on the alert, stand firm in the faith,
act like men, be strong.
Let all that you do be done in love."

I CORINTHIANS 16:13-14

BOLDNESS is an attitude of strong confidence in God, such that godly things are said and done openly without fear of the consequences. How can we be encouraged to make the decision to act boldly today? A bold life is a decision. There's never a better time to make the commitment to live boldly than today. In Proverbs, there's a verse about being bold as a lion. The analogy speaks to strength, courage, and dominance.

"The wicked flee when no one is pursuing,
but the righteous are bold as a lion."

PROVERBS 28:1

THE RIGHTEOUS ARE BOLD

"Since therefore, brethren, we have confidence to enter the holy place
by the blood of Jesus, by a new and living way
which He inaugurated for us through the veil, that is,
His flesh, and since we have a great high priest
over the house of God, let us draw near with a sincere heart in full assurance
of faith, having our hearts sprinkled clean from an evil conscience and our
bodies washed with clean water.
Let us hold fast to the confession of our hope
without ever wavering, for He who promised is faithful;
and let us consider how to stimulate one another
to love and good deeds, not forsaking our own assembling together,
as is the habit of some, but encouraging one another;
and all the more, as you see the day drawing near."

HEBREWS 10:19-25

OUR MISSION IS CLEAR.

READING THIS, THERE CAN BE NO DOUBT

AS TO WHAT WE'VE BEEN CALLED TO DO.

LET US NOT WAVER!
BE BOLD!

TABLE OF CONTENTS

BOLD AND BEYOND 121

BOLD IN THE BIBLE 177

PROLOGUE

THE JOURNEY TO BOLDNESS

We all had a year in 2020 like none other, and I don't think anyone could have predicted what would happen. Those of us in the book business, or any business, had to go with the flow and morph our work into something that would fit the times and give us a way to still keep afloat. I had had a new book released the previous summer and had all sorts of scheduled events ...which were all canceled. After a busy fall in 2019, I just assumed things would continue.

I went to a media conference the month before the pandemic hit and had some great interviews. I was stoked. Two weeks later, our state shut down. Of course, we all thought it would be done by summer. Nope. I started having some self-doubt about how to continue my ministry, and by September, when all events were canceled and book sales slowed, I was a tad discouraged. I had a friend ask me to what end would I continue this ministry? I am sixty-two.

I still have a list of books I want to create, and an inner desire and calling to share my faith with as many people as possible. The more I thought about it, the more I felt motivated to continue despite the circumstances.

I prayed about it and knew in my heart that I was to continue. How would God allow so many miraculous things to happen in my life, and then want me to not share His love with everyone? I looked over the outlines for a couple of the books I "thought" would be next and was not sure what to do. One thought kept surfacing in my mind .... one foot in front of the other; purposefully move forward. I knew instinctively that God would bring clarity, as He had so many times before.

At the media conference the previous year, one word kept coming up, "intentionally." I had several radio and TV interviews, and in answering some questions, I kept using that word, "intention." My second book was about helping others, reaching out, and welcoming others. I thought about how we must CHOOSE to do what God wants us to do. We have to take action. I thought of the pandemic, earthquakes, fires, floods, and death. So many people were so scared and wondered what was going on. Is the world coming to an end? How long will this all last?

Then it came to me: toss aside the other book ideas for now and give readers a book relevant for today. I fiddled with title ideas and talked to my team, and we decided that BOLDNESS was so important right now. People need hope and some guidance. I hope we can all share God's love with others so they can feel comforted and know that the Gospel can give them that hope. If we are to accomplish anything, we need to speak out boldly with the hope God gives us. There is no better time for the truth.

Our home group Bible study has been doing a video series on Greece and Paul's missionary journeys there. If anyone was purposeful and bold, it was Paul. He continued to go where he knew he must, no matter what he was up against. He pushed forward. He knew he had to do what God asked of him. He might be beaten, run out of town, or put in prison, but he moved forward with intention.

How can each one of us make the decision to boldly do and say what God has asked of each one of us?

Our discouragement from the events that occurred during this pandemic should not cause us to shut down, but should inspire us to encourage those around us and to share the good news of the gospel.

Matthew 28:18-20 is often referred to as the Great Commission. Jesus is telling His disciples to go and tell the gospel to everyone, "all nations." Jesus knew He would no longer be with them on earth and commissioned them to share the gospel.

> *"And Jesus came up and spoke to them, saying,*
> *All authority has been given to Me in Heaven and on earth.*
> *Go therefore and make disciples of all nations,*
> *baptizing them in the name of the Father and the Son*
> *and the Holy Spirit, teaching them to observe*
> *all that I commanded you;*
> *and lo, I am with you always,*
> *even to the end of the age."*

"All authority" points to Jesus' deity; "even to the end of the age" shows us He will always be with us. Therefore, I believe He is also instructing all believers, not just the disciples, to share their faith.

I love this passage in Romans 10:13-15.

> *"for whoever will call upon the name of the Lord will be saved.*
> *How then shall they call upon Him in whom they have not believed?*
> *And how shall they believe in Him whom they have not heard?*

And how shall they hear without a preacher?
And how shall they preach unless they are sent?
Just as it is written, 'How beautiful are the feet of those
who bring glad tidings of good things!"

Paul uses these rhetorical questions to point out that hearing the Gospel message precedes saving faith. He uses the Word to reveal the salvation God grants, which is saving faith to everyone who believes in His Gospel.

We can pray for God to give us a burden for others so that we feel a sense of urgency to share our faith with others. We have a great opportunity to serve God boldly. At the very least, it is a requirement as a Christian to share this truth with others.

We have missionary friends. We have followed their ministry for the past twenty-eight years. Many times, when they are home to the states, we try to get together. They have been the most inspirational people to me. They are the greatest example to me of being bold for their faith. They work in a very dangerous area of the world. I do not want to hinder their ministry in any way, but wanted to share a couple instances that will give you an idea of how they live and are constantly thinking of living with intention and purpose.

One time when this man was visiting us, we took him out for dinner at Texas Roadhouse. As we were leaving, I informed him that this location was the busiest intersection in the entire state of Idaho. He looked across the street and asked why we didn't have a church there. Always thinking with purpose. It really got me thinking, he is right, why don't we? Another instance is remembering how he waited in front of a large institution for months, every day, until they finally told him that they could hold Bible studies inside the building. Every day for months. That is determination. That is what this book is about. When I asked if they could contribute to a chapter for this book, I knew they were too busy and I knew it might be dangerous. I understood they could not do it. I told them that they were my inspiration for this book because they have always been bold for Christ, no matter the consequences or how dangerous. And he said, "And we will always continue to be." That, my friends, is my reason for writing this book.

In this book, I will highlight believers who purposely moved in a direction that may have seemed risky—maybe out of their comfort zone—but they knew God wanted them to serve in mighty ways. They intentionally put their plan into action, just like Paul, who kept going no matter the obstacles. I chose these people because I have always admired them and the path they have taken. These models of boldness exemplify various people from the Bible, and I will explore passages of scripture that relate to their story.

There will also be examples of bold faith of people who have been used by God who have lived in the past. And then finally, there will be more examples from scripture of Bible characters who bravely stood against all odds for God.

I am excited about this book and hope it inspires you to be bold, live intentionally, and follow through on your goals to share the good news of Jesus to the ends of the earth.

"And he stayed two full years in his own rented quarters,
and was welcoming all who came to him,
preaching the kingdom of God,
and teaching concerning the Lord Jesus Christ
with all openness, unhindered."

ACTS 28:30-31

"Let us therefore draw near with confidence
to the throne of grace,
that we may receive mercy and may find grace
to help in time of need."

HEBREWS 4:16

"For God has not given us a spirit of timidity,
but of power and love and discipline."

1 TIMOTHY 1:7

Intention: 1. a thing intended; an aim or plan

2. the action of intending

"The Lord is my light and my salvation,
whom shall I fear?
The Lord is the stronghold of my life,
of whom shall I be afraid?"

PSALM 27:1 (ESV)

I HAVE BUT ONE CANDLE OF LIFE TO BURN. AND I WOULD RATHER BURN IT OUT IN A LAND FILLED WITH DARKNESS THAN IN A LAND FLOODED WITH LIGHT.
- ION KEITH-FALCONER

CHAPTER 1

Gabrielle

God Put it into My Heart

How can you boldly serve God wherever you are? I was so excited to receive the following testimony from this young woman who has accomplished so much in her life. She is a great example of someone being bold in their faith and life. I have watched her grow up and stand for truth and be extremely motivated and focused. Gabrielle's experience will inspire you.

Gabrielle

"God has called me to glorify Him as I fight human trafficking."

I fell in love with law in high school, but I was immediately unsure how to pursue a career in law that would honor God. After all, lawyer stereotypes make it clear that lawyers are greedy and self-centered and they capitalize on other people's misery. So how could I be a lawyer and serve God's kingdom, not my own?

I raised the question in a Bible study, and some friends mentioned the tragedy of human trafficking. In that moment, God planted a seed in my heart. About two years later, I watched a documentary on international sex trafficking. It absolutely broke my heart. I prayed that night, committing myself to the mission of fighting sex trafficking. "God," I prayed, "I believe this is what you want me to do, so this is what I'm aiming for. If this isn't Your plan for me, I need you to redirect me."

That has been my mentality ever since. I call it my pinball philosophy: I am a pinball rocketing through a pinball machine, and God wholeheartedly directs me as He desires. Instead of refusing to move until after He illuminates all the steps, I will start running in faith as soon as I sense Him nudging me in a particular direction. If He redirects me, I refuse to see that as a failure on my part. My wisdom is small and His is infinite, so I will keep advancing as He shapes and reshapes my life.

With my new calling in mind, I ran hard. Enabled by God's blessing, I graduated in four years with three degrees, including a Master's in Political Science. I wrote my thesis on international human trafficking, planning to start law school immediately afterwards. However, I did not yet know where I should attend law school. I prayed, and I made a list of my favorite schools. But God, as He often does, directed me somewhere totally different. And He did not direct me in a pleasant way.

The summer before taking the LSAT, I was forced to stop running. A domino effect of broken situations brought me to a place of deep depression. Losing faith in God's love for me, I flinched away from the very thought that He had a plan for my life. After all, His plans clearly allowed for too much pain. In a fog of depression, I found myself wandering through a law school fair filled with representatives from various schools. I wasn't excited or optimistic or curious—I didn't feel anything.

Then an admissions director from Nevada's one and only law school jumped out from around his table to talk to me, explaining the many opportunities the school could provide for someone like me to fight sex trafficking. In that instant, I knew where I was going to law school. God had once again proven Himself faithful to direct me.

He continued providing for me, again and again. From scholarships to housing, from success in school itself to incredible connections with people and organizations. And again and again, God has confirmed His calling on my life.

During my three years of law school, I walked the Las Vegas Strip, reaching out to sex workers overlooked by everyone but those wanting to use them, praying with them on the streets at three in the morning. I responded to calls from victim-survivors of sex trafficking desperate to escape an abusive relationship. I loved young girls who've been through more horrors in their short lives than I can wrap my head around. I wrote a bill to eliminate the statute of limitations for sex trafficking offenses and, when it was sponsored by an assemblywoman, presented an amended version before the Nevada legislature.

It's breathtaking. It's heartbreaking. It's too big for me. Whenever I'm tempted to pull back and live a more comfortable life, God shows me how empty it is to pursue anything but His vision for me. Whenever other things try to distract me, God restores to me an undivided heart. And even when sin clouds my eyes, God remains faithful.

I think of the story of the prophet Nehemiah. He was a cupbearer to the king of Persia when he learned of a tragedy: Jerusalem's wall was broken, leaving the people vulnerable and the city in disgrace. Nehemiah didn't wait for someone to give him direction; he believed that his desire to rebuild the wall could only come from God. He prayed for success, which God granted again and again—first in directing the king to send Nehemiah to Jerusalem, then in enabling Nehemiah and the workers to rebuild the wall, then in fighting for Nehemiah against fierce opposition, both physical attacks and insidious scheming. No matter what new trouble arose to distract Nehemiah, he devoted himself to the work because God was sustaining him.

At one point, men who opposed Nehemiah's work tried to convince him to meet with them so they could harm him, but Nehemiah was steadfast. He replied, *"I am doing a great work and I cannot come down. Why should the work stop while I leave it and come down to you?"* He knew what God's calling for him was, and everything else paled to insignificance in comparison. And the surrounding nations saw that the work had been done with the help of God.

I want to be single-minded like that. I pray that no obstacle or temptation ever causes me to leave the great work God has called me to do, just as He has called all of us to great works. He is thrilled to share His mission with His children, and what an honor it is to be co-laborers with Christ.

WHAT STEPS CAN YOU TAKE

IN YOUR OWN LIFE

TO BECOME MORE INTENTIONAL?

This amazing young woman who just shared her story is only twenty-four years old. She has a God-given goal and follows through. As a matter of fact, she exceeds what the goal even was in the first place as she listens, hears, and takes action. She is not fearful, she is not timid, and she is definitely not complacent.

Not all of us can rebuild a city wall or create a bill for the legislature. But we can follow through on our current goals and we can shine for Christ to those around us. What has God put into your heart? Whatever it is, He will give you the strength, power, and means to continue on.

ONE DOES NOT SURRENDER A LIFE IN
AN INSTANT. THAT WHICH IS LIFELONG
CAN ONLY BE SURRENDERED
IN A LIFETIME.
– JIM ELLIOT

CHAPTER 2

Sam

Growth Through Mentoring

MANY OF US HAVE THOSE PEOPLE IN OUR LIVES

WHO SPEAK TRUTH INTO US.

A mentor provides truth in love, and leadership. It could be that they correct you or call you out on things because they love you, or it might be that they're there when you need instruction, or it could be spiritual discipleship. Mentors are critical to success.

For the past fifty years, I have been involved in various roles of some form of the above. And someone who fills that main role is still in my life. She has directed me, scolded me gently, and laughed and cried with me. I have looked to her for guidance when I had no clue what to do. I have tried to also reach out to those who may need someone in their life in that role as well.

The following testimony is from my brother-in-law. I met him in 1976. I drove to a college career day for the college my sister attended, and I remember meeting Sam very clearly. It was homecoming at the college, and it was 1950s night. Sam, who had a rather rugged look about him, had on his leather jacket and totally looked the part. Sam was a basketball star at Los Angeles Baptist College and Seminary, now The Master's University. He actually still holds many of their top ten records. He, by his own admission, was not a studious person at that time in his life. Everything about Sam, then and now too, was about *relationship.* I was starstruck. He spoke with almost a slight speech impediment, and I thought he was the coolest. I was so happy for my sister. They got married in 1977, and as I got to know Sam more and more through the years I could see through his life the things that were important to him. He values people and God.

Two things impress me. First, he is still all about *relationship.* He used to talk to his dad for four hours on the phone. That was shocking to me. And he had all these guys he was spending time with, which leads us to the second thing. He shares the gospel with almost everyone. He has led many to Christ. He is not fearful. God gave him a loud booming voice. He can go into his hometown hardware store and everyone knows him. He smiles and greets them. This is just who he is. He used to go to Starbucks every day, and everyone knew him. He would sit and study and talk to people. He is all about *relationship.*

It does not surprise me that this is what he chose to tell us about. He values people. He wants to be teachable and seeks those he can learn from.

He felt humbled and inadequate to write this story for me. But life happens to us all, and while we see ourselves as imperfect, God can use our life stories to encourage others.

2 TIMOTHY 2:1-2 READS,

"You therefore, my son,
be strong in the grace that is in Christ Jesus.

And the things which you have heard from me
in the presence of many witnesses,
these entrust to faithful men,
who will be able to teach others also."

For many years being a Christian I have often wondered and observed why some Christians seem to be more engaged and active in their faith, while other Christians are less so. After all, we know that all true believers have received the gift of the Holy Spirit. The Spirit is the "power of God". The working of the Holy Spirit is what Paul refers to in Ephesians 1:19, *"....and what is the immeasurable greatness of his power towards us who believe, according to the working of his great might."*

Ever since as a young boy I received Jesus as my Savior, I experienced this "working" of the Holy Spirit in my life. The Spirit has always been active, motivating in various ways. There have been times when I would resist this power, due to willful disobedience, but at the end of the day or sometimes for longer periods, the Spirit always got its way. (Praise God). Being a Christian is synonymous to being filled and empowered by the Holy Spirit; but there is a duality (yin and yang) to one's motivation in cultivating one's faith.

Apostle Paul writing to young Timothy says *"For this reason I remind you to fan into flame the gift of God, which is in you through the laying of my hands, for God gave us a spirit not of fear but of power and love and self-control"* (2 Timothy 1:6-7) The way I experienced how this worked in my own faith journey, is that God provides the fire (my gift) but I need to "fan" that flame. The way I have done this has been by taking advantage of being discipled by older Godly men, leading by example, in their own spiritual formation, teaching me how to study God's word, how to pray and share my faith. There has been nothing more effective in my Christian maturity other than the Spirit itself, than to be in a Paul/Timothy relationship.

Having been discipled gave me a lifelong thirst for God's word which has proven to be the most effective way in fanning the "gift of God" in my life. When I fan the "flame" my fears become less and his power of love and self-control becomes a greater force in my life.

Discipleship is a way of training others so they can also train others. Teaching others about Christ helps them to share their faith. You are walking alongside them, encouraging them to grow.

I love the relationship between Paul and Timothy in the New Testament. Timothy was from Lystra, a city in the province of Galatia. We read in 1 Timothy 1:2,

"to Timothy, my true child in the faith..."

referencing that Paul had led Timothy to Christ, most likely on his first missionary journey. Then, on his second journey, he had Timothy accompany him. Paul mentored and taught Timothy and discipled him. Timothy was Paul's helper in ministry, friend, and companion. When Paul was in his final days, he asked Timothy to come to him before he died. In 2 Timothy 4:9, Paul says,

"Make every effort to come to me soon;"

Then, in verse 21, he says again,

"Make every effort to come before winter."

He loved Timothy so much. He wanted to pass the baton of his ministry, and you can sense the urgency in his letter.

I would encourage you to find a mentor and be discipled by someone, like Sam was. And also, to reach out to someone to mentor. I love this passage in 1 Corinthians. It is an example of us living intentionally and sharing Christ with those around us. 1 Corinthians 3:5-10,

"What then is Apollos, are you not mere men?
And what is Paul? Servants through whom you believed,
even as the Lord gave opportunity to each one.
I planted, Apollos watered, but God was causing the growth.
So then neither the one who plants nor the one who waters
is anything, but God causes the growth.
Now he who plants and he who waters are one;
but each will receive his own reward according to his own labor.
For we are God's fellow workers; you are God's fellow workers;
you are God's field, God's building.
According to the grace of God which was given me,
as a wise master builder I laid a foundation

and another is building upon it.
But let each man be careful how he builds upon it."

Discipleship matters, no matter how old or young you are. How can you find a mentor, and be one, today? You and I may just be a small piece to the puzzle in this vast universe, and that's okay. You can still help someone, reach out, befriend an unlikely person, share your life, share your faith, and then teach others to grow in their spiritual life. I have had the opportunity several times to spend time with younger women, and each time, it feels orchestrated by God. It doesn't always have to be something that needs a big thought-out action plan, or weekly message or study. Sometimes, it can just be going to a coffee shop and listening to them share about their life and what is happening. I have gone on long walks with people, gone to lunch, worked on projects, and even shared my own struggles. You don't need to be superhuman to them, you just need to be real. If they think you are perfect, then they will be hesitant to share openly with you. In your own life, remember to disciple others and to find someone spiritually yoked to disciple you.

I have had people show up at my door late at night needing to talk, and it's a great thing when it occurs because they know I will sacrifice my time for them. Being available is so important. I have seen this time and time again in Sam's life, and he has been a great example to me.

DO GOOD: AS WE HAVE TIME, AND OPPORTUNITY, TO DO GOOD IN EVERY POSSIBLE KIND, AND IN EVERY POSSIBLE DEGREE TO ALL MEN.
- JOHN WESLEY

CHAPTER 3

Dale and Elisabeth

Intentional Care

Are you hearing God clearly?

In order to serve God,

we must first hear His plan

for what He wants us to do.

There are times when He will move you

to take action even when you

were not planning to.

Sometimes, we just need to meet the needs of others. It may not be a convenient time or place, but we need to do whatever it takes. Perhaps someone has come to your home at midnight needing a place to stay, or they have run away from home. Will we turn them away? I hope not. Time and time again, we may see opportunities to give someone respite away from their burdens, provide meals, or just be a friend by spending time with them. Scripture gives us many examples of this, including a man named Stephanas.

In 1 Corinthians 16:14-18, we learn that Stephanas and others ministered to Paul, and you can tell how much this meant to Paul. It reads,

"Let all that you do be done in love.
Now I urge you, brethren
(you know that the household of Stephanas,
that they were the first fruits of Achaia, and that they
have devoted themselves for ministry to the saints),
that you also be in subjection to such men
and to everyone who helps in the work and labors.
I rejoice over the coming of Stephanas and Fortunatus and Achaicus; because they have supplied what was lacking on your part.
For they have refreshed my spirit and yours.
Therefore acknowledge such men."

These members of the household of Stephanas were some of the first believers in Corinth in Southern Greece. They were visiting Paul in Ephesus (located in modern Turkey) when Paul was writing his letter to the Corinthians. Paul was happy to see his friends and spend time with them.

I love people opening their homes to others. We have done this many times through the years, not only to help them, but it also ministers to us and blesses us. The following testimony comes from a family we were fortunate to have in our home for a couple of weeks during a missions conference. They had three of their kids with them, and we were so fortunate to get to know them. I have to admit that when I asked them to write this, I totally thought they would talk about their ministry in missions because it is an awesome and rather extreme ministry. However, I am pleased that their missions ministry, while a big part of their life, was not what they chose to share, but they shared about the legacy from their parents and to their kids in regard to ministering to the saints. This is something so near and dear to my heart.

Dale and Elisabeth

From a young age, we both saw our parents living intentional, unashamed lives for the glory of God. Dale experienced this as a missionary kid while his parents served at a small mission hospital on a remote, tropical island in the Pacific. Elisabeth saw this also growing up on the mission field in a more developed country where her parents served at a church and servicemen's center. Intentional hospitality and sacrificial care for others became a significant piece of the fabric of our lives and played an important role in what our ministry became after we got married. When you grow up watching models who lived intentional, live-what-I teach lives, it is not difficult to follow their examples because that's the only way you know how to live. When we began our own ministry together as a missionary family, being intentional was not even something we really thought about ...we just did it.

We paid the airfare for other missionaries to come visit us knowing that they needed to get away from the pressures and stress of the concrete jungle where they served. We had fellow language students in our home during the holidays because we knew they were alone with no teammates in the country. We drove an hour just to have prayer time with fellow missionaries because we knew if we needed it that they probably needed it too. We made time to listen to fellow missionaries who were burned out, discouraged and just needed a listening ear. Time and again we opened our home for meals with those who just needed fellowship. And games! There is no better way we have found to connect and build relationships with people than to play a good board game around the dining room table. Most people are so busy they don't have time for fun and fellowship. It's "water to a thirsty soul" to just laugh and enjoy games with one another.

Just before Christmas one year we became instant foster parents for five siblings while their parents were going through a difficult separation. It was all-hands-on-deck for the entire family during one typhoon as an exhausted missionary family arrived unexpectedly and needed a place to shelter from the storm and sleep before continuing on their journey. We scrambled to make beds and provide a warm meal for them in spite of the lateness of the hour. Numerous times, we "gave up" personal family time to minister to the needs of the broader family of Christ knowing that at that moment, God wanted us to care for a brother or sister in need. We opened our ministry facility to a family visiting our city who needed a place to stay so they wouldn't have to worry about bed bugs, spiders or other unwanted critters at the place they had intended to stay.

Honestly, doing the little things that were not a big deal to us seemed to bring the biggest impact in caring for God's people. It was buying groceries for a family because God had blessed us, and we wanted to share it. It was taking others on our family vacations so they could have a chance to see God's beautiful creation that always soothed our souls. To us, the more the merrier! But to others, inviting them to be a part of our family blessed their socks off! It really doesn't take much, but it does take being observant to the needs around you and finding creative ways to intentionally care for people. It's so easy to be inward-focused, and protect ourselves, our time and our families. Yet, we can attest to the fact that when you reach out to include, help, and care for others (especially those in ministry), you end up being the one who is blessed. Devote yourselves to the service of the saints!

"They have devoted themselves to the service of the saints."

1 CORINTHIANS 16:15

It is so easy nowadays with our fast-paced lives to be caught up in everyday life. We have work, family, church, errands, the list goes on and on. I would challenge you to look beyond your everyday activities. Look around you and observe the lives around you. See the needs around you and how you can minister to someone else.

Boldly offer your time to others. I guarantee they will be thankful, and even if they say no, they will know that you care. Many times someone who is overwhelmed with life just needs rest. Young moms can be too tired to cope. When I had my first child I had a close friend who came at about nine or ten in the evening and would walk the baby so I could just sit for a while. She also did ironing, cooked meals and took us on errands to fun places, like craft stores.

By intentionally caring for others, we can refresh their spirit. Perhaps this means taking time from your busy schedule to invite someone to join you on a walk, bike ride, trip to the grocery store or a baking day. Time away doing something different often provides refreshment to the spirit for someone who may be going through a tough time. A little time away or cup of coffee with a neighbor may be exactly what they need. One of our children has a chronic illness. It was an every day, every week, and every month thing. Being invited and going to have dinner or to a game night at someone's house was a blessing to us. I am very thankful for the help and friendship from those who reached out to our family.

I love having people stay with us when they are passing through. It is an easy thing to do, even if you don't have a guest room and a great help to your guests. For years, we just put people on our hide-a-bed. We have had a guest room the past several years, so I just make sure it is always ready. As soon as someone leaves, I wash the sheets so it is ready for the next guest. If you keep it low-key, then people do not feel they are a burden. I also tell them they can come and go as they please. I don't want them to feel awkward at all but that they can kick their shoes off and be at home. We have had people stay for multiple weeks so maybe they want to do laundry or cook their own meals. That's great too. We don't need to micromanage someone we are trying to help because God will take them the rest of the way. Be open and flexible.

I have so many friends who have taken care of or are currently taking care of an aging parent. This is exhausting, both emotionally and physically, not just because of the physical aspect of staying up all night but because of the emotional aspects of watching someone you love dearly decline. It clenches our hearts and shakes the foundation of who we are. I watched my sister take care of our mom for decades. While they lived in two separate houses on the same farm, my sister would often sleep at my mom's house so she could hear her if there was a problem. She made sure our mom had help if she needed to get up at night or needed to get to her medicine. I do not think my sister slept soundly for years. She sat endless nights and listened to our mom read her nightly devotions. Usually, it was a Bible passage, her Corrie ten Boom book, and Our Daily Bread. I am sure this blessed my sister as she blessed our mom with her help and presence.

Time spent with someone is exactly what God wants of us. The gift of time is a critical commodity in helping others, yet often we underestimate the value of it, especially if it's with a stranger. We can find ways to minister to those close to us just by being there for them, and to strangers, as well.

Try to remember that even though you might not see the results, still try to find ways to minister to others. Pray for opportunities if you aren't quite sure how to go about this. We all have busy schedules and it is very easy to go about our week and not include anyone else to help, seek out or talk to, but one way is to include someone in your already planned activity. If I am going to take a young friend out for coffee sometimes it is thoughtful to invite their friend too. It shows the person that you are interested in them on a different level, and casts a wide net. You also get to know the person better and maybe you will discover a new need that you can meet. Get in their world, just like Jesus did.

Be in the right place at the right time, and you'll experience true joy from helping others, as a byproduct of the time invested, and spent. Most of the time it ministers to us in an amazing way. I have been abundantly blessed by helping others and so will you.

HERE THEN IS THE GREAT TRUTH. IN THE PAIN. THE AGONY. AND THE HEROIC ENDEAVORS OF LIFE. WE PASS THROUGH A REFINER'S FIRE. AND THE INSIGNIFICANT AND THE UNIMPORTANT IN OUR LIVES CAN MELT AWAY LIKE DROSS AND MAKE OUR FAITH BRIGHT. INTACT. AND STRONG.
- JAMES E. FAUST

CHAPTER 4

Curtis and Deanne

In the Middle of the Fire

There are many instances in the Bible of where God used those who had gone through trials to save the lives of others. Curtis and Deanne are one couple who have faced many trials and yet are still obedient to God. This couple has had a rough go and bad news on top of bad news, with a long road ahead, and yet they have shown the love of Christ and shared the hope of salvation with everyone they have met. I truly believe God will reward them for their faithfulness.

Their young daughter went in for a routine outpatient procedure and her heart was perforated. They did CPR for fifteen minutes and although she is alive, she will probably have a long road of recovery ahead of her and life will never be the same. This event and news would devastate anyone. The dreams you had for your daughter, the hopes for her future flashing before your eyes as they go down the drain. But this couple has stood firm in their love of God and preach His faithfulness and love to anyone who will listen. Their story is touching not only those around them, but people across the country and the world as they have posted updates on social media and asked people to pray. They have been an inspiration to everyone, and God's name is being glorified. They are a living example of how we cannot control what occurs to us, but we can control how we reply and react when God wants to work through us.

This doesn't mean that every day has been wonderful or that they have always felt that they are responding perfectly, but God is doing a work in them and through them. Their boldness to constantly and purposefully share the gospel with the nurses, doctors, and hospital workers has stood out to those around them and those around the world.

Curtis and Deanne

Do you ever go through your days with no excitement or seemingly pointless interactions? Do you feel blah and ever ask yourself what happened to the excitement or anticipation of life? I think if we are all honest, we could say yes to the aforementioned questions from time to time. And if we are not careful and proactive, that time to time can quickly become the everyday normal.

So how do we fight to continue to have purpose? Remember that God is near not distant, acting not passive, moving not still, and desiring to partner with you—not have you on the sidelines. Hear these verses.

"For if, while we were enemies, we were reconciled to God
through the death of His Son, then how much more, having
been reconciled, will we be saved by His life! And not only that,
but we also rejoice in God through our Lord Jesus Christ.
We have now received this reconciliation through Him."

ROMANS 5:10-11 HCSB

"Therefore, if anyone is in Christ, he is a new creation;
old things have passed away, and look, new things have come.
Everything is from God, who reconciled us to Himself
through Christ and gave us the ministry of reconciliation:
That is, in Christ, God was reconciling the world to Himself,
not counting their trespasses against them,
and He has committed the message of reconciliation to us.
Therefore, we are ambassadors for Christ, certain that God
is appealing through us. We plead on Christ's behalf,
"Be reconciled to God." He made the One
who did not know sin to be sin for us,
so that we might become the righteousness of God in Him."

2 CORINTHIANS 5:17-21 HCSB

"For you were called to this, because Christ also suffered for you,
leaving you an example, so that you should follow in His steps.
He did not commit sin, and no deceit was found in His mouth;
when He was reviled, He did not revile in return;
when He was suffering, He did not threaten
but entrusted Himself to the One who judges justly.
He Himself bore our sins in His body on the tree, so that,
having died to sins, we might live for righteousness;
you have been healed by His wounds.
For you were like sheep going astray,
but you have now returned to the Shepherd
and Guardian of your souls."

1 PETER 2:21-25 HCSB

"So rid yourselves of all malice, all deceit, hypocrisy, envy, and all slander. Like newborn infants, desire the pure spiritual milk, so that you may grow by it for your salvation, since you have tasted that the Lord is good. Coming to Him, a living stone—rejected by men but chosen and valuable to God—you yourselves, as living stones, are being built into a spiritual house for a holy priesthood to offer spiritual sacrifices acceptable to God through Jesus Christ."

1 Peter 2:1-5 HCSB

"For this very reason, make every effort to supplement your faith with goodness, goodness with knowledge, knowledge with self-control, self-control with endurance, endurance with godliness, godliness with brotherly affection, and brotherly affection with love. For if these qualities are yours and are increasing, they will keep you from being useless or unfruitful in the knowledge of our Lord Jesus Christ. The person who lacks these things is blind and shortsighted and has forgotten the cleansing from his past sins. Therefore, brothers, make every effort to confirm your calling and election, because if you do these things you will never stumble. For in this way, entry into the eternal kingdom of our Lord and Savior Jesus Christ will be richly supplied to you."

2 Peter 1:5-11 HCSB

So take those verses and ask yourself how can I implement some of them into my daily journey. A good teacher finds a story in every situation. They are actively looking for the good works in which God has prepared for them. Every interaction becomes an opportunity.

But you say that that is exhausting, that's too much work. Is it? Is it really more exhausting than the bleak meaningless and mind numbing nothingness of not really going after it? Just think back to the times in your life when you were a part of something that was bigger than yourself. A sports team, a project, a mission trip. Remember how utterly tired you were and yet remarkably energized.

You see, when you go to the Grand Canyon you don't go there to see how big and magnanimous you are. You go there to feel how small you are. There is something magical about knowing and feeling and understanding that you are not at the center of the universe. That you are actually so very small but a part of the greatest adventure and story that has ever been told.

So here are some practical tips for staying effective and purposeful:

Conversations: in every conversation you have, attempt to be able to answer one of these 3 questions. 1) Did they learn something more about Jesus? 2) Are they encouraged to live and love Jesus more? 3) Did you listen and try to meet a need through the power of the Spirit?

Mundane Tasks: attempt to see, know and experience that God is using those small things to help shape you, to give you time to reflect and pray, to build your stamina. Understand that it is in the mundane that habits for big things are built.

Driving: Use this time to think about God. Sometimes just in silence. Make ministry-minded phone calls. Listen to worship music. Listen to the Bible. Listen to books. Don't waste your commute. For some of us this could be 2+ hours a day.

Leisure times: Play hard. Enjoy using your body to have fun, and enjoy the ability to walk and run and play. The Puritans talked about holy leisure. God wants us to enjoy life and glorify Him in all we do.

Easter-egg-hunt living: Because God has preordained good works in advance for you to do, this gives you an ability to live each day differently and purposely. Keep your eyes open and your heart ready to see that anything and everything can become something big!

God is sovereign: Finally, when you know and recognize that your days are numbered. Knowing that you can't add or subtract one moment to the span of your life gives you the freedom to live life boldly and passionately. You don't have to live in fear. God's got this.

Now the real goal is to put the scriptures into practice each day. We will fail, I promise you that, but our loving heavenly Father is right there to pick you up, dust you off, and with a gentle and loving pat on the back remind you to, "have fun my child. This is the day I have made. Rejoice and be glad in it."

HAVE YOU EVER ACTED INTENTIONALLY LIKE THEY DO? PERHAPS YOU HAVE, BUT I KNOW I CAN LEARN A LOT FROM THEIR STORY.

How I wish I had boldness like this. Curtis's practical ways to be bold and purposeful are so helpful. I have every confidence God will reward his faithfulness. Already, his daughter's ICU nurse has come to know Christ as her personal Savior. If nothing else comes of this, that will be enough. Praise God!

Sometimes when you are in the middle of the fire, in the midst of a trial, it is hard to keep your focus. It makes it hard to stay bold and purposeful because you naturally go into survival mode. But God can give you the strength and help you to stay focused on Him. In the end, you'll see the purpose to your pain.

This testimony was submitted by Jessica Everett

THERE ARE MANY OF US THAT ARE WILLING TO DO GREAT THINGS FOR THE LORD. BUT FEW OF US ARE WILLING TO DO LITTLE THINGS.
- D.L. MOODY

CHAPTER 5

Cosmo and Sarah

Willing to Serve

ARE YOU WILLING TO SERVE?

Servant leaders are willing, so when the opportunity presents itself, they go. They go and they do and they help change the lives of others. I know Sarah through my oldest daughter who worked for our local rescue mission as a grant writer. Sarah is also an administrator for the rescue mission, managing six locations. She is busy for Christ and accomplishes so much, fully embracing what God has given her to do even if it doesn't look like what she expected years ago.

Cosmo and Sarah

I am quiet; Cosmo has been blessed with a loud voice. I prefer to read; Cosmo is natural with people and is a compelling storyteller. I am from sunny Southern California; Cosmo is from a small village in Northeast India that has no running water. What we have in common, besides our love for one another and God, is a deep, abiding desire to see people come to know the love of our God and His saving grace.

Cosmo and I met in Bangkok, Thailand in 1998 at a conference for Christian sports ministers. We were both sports ministers (using sports as a platform to share the Gospel) – he taught martial arts in India and I was a missionary who coached basketball and taught English in Hong Kong. We dated long distance for a few years and married in the United States in 2002, moving to Idaho a few weeks later.

Initially, we felt out of place in Idaho. I was in a different state and Cosmo was in an entirely different country. We found jobs, bought a house, and settled into life. Yet, we missed the ministry we were a part of in Asia. After a few years, Cosmo and I opened up a martial arts school (dojo) in Downtown Nampa. We began to see why God led us to Idaho and how He can use martial arts to bring people into His Kingdom.

God brings in kids, teens, and adults who are going through a lot of trials and hardships. Kids who have been bullied come into the school and their parents want us to help them develop confidence and boost their self-esteem. Shy students come in to learn how to be leaders. Youth and young adults who are in gangs and are at-risk are drawn to the dojo or they are referred by a counselor, pastor, police, or probation officer. Alongside the martial arts training, we also teach basic principles like respect, discipline and serving. As part of the leadership or mentor program, students may have to clean the dojo or wipe the toilets. We also teach simple concepts like how to respect women. Many of these youth have never cleaned a toilet or learned to respect women in a Biblical way. Eventually, we teach them about the purpose of life through Christ.

Some of the youth want to know more and we gather into small groups for Bible studies and discipleship. We have seen some of our students give their hearts to God. When they want to get baptized, we bring a horse trough to the school and baptize them, or a local church opens their baptismal for us to use.

Cosmo and I have failed many times in our attempts to help people, yet our hearts are filled with compassion. In our frustration, we sometimes tell the teens to leave, but they want to keep coming back. We have learned to love them and speak truth into their lives during training or by simply hanging out. We use what we have to bring glory to God and people into His Kingdom. It's not much, but God uses the martial arts school for His glory.

Through the dojo and our friends, we are also blessing India. Since Cosmo is from a village that does not have basic necessities, he knows how much a quality education helps provide a future and a hope to children. We took over the management of a small, floundering school in his home village. We formed a nonprofit to support that Christian school and also began helping widows, single moms, and people in ministry to start small business ventures to support themselves (and they also give a portion of their profits to the school). Last year, we opened a second school in another village to ensure children in five surrounding villages are able to have a Christian and English-speaking education.

At times, the ministries in India and (in the beginning) the martial arts school were overwhelming. We wondered how the two of us could do everything. On paper, it looks like a lot, but God has surrounded us with people who can help us fulfill this vision. It's all for Him and we give it back to Him. All He desires from us is obedience, to make the time for Him and be available. That's all He asks.

It is true that is what He asks of us. The prophet Isaiah also entered ministry. Things seemed a little overwhelming to him. He wanted to do all God had set before him, but was hesitant at first.

The name Isaiah means **"The Lord is salvation."** Isaiah is quoted directly in the New Testament over sixty-five times, far more than any other Old Testament prophet and mentioned by name over twenty times. He prophesied to the Israelites before the Babylonian captivity because of their departure from the Lord. In Isaiah chapter six, God calls Isaiah to serve Him. Isaiah is so overwhelmed by God's holiness that he is distraught over his own sin and the soon-to-be prophet feels convicted. This is a good thing as Isaiah is commissioned into ministry. He is fully aware of his sin, he is humbled, and he knows God has chosen him. The key here is that Isaiah was willing. In Isaiah 6:8, he says,

> *"Also I heard the voice of the Lord, saying,*
> *'Whom shall I send, and who will go for Us?'*
> *Then I said 'Here am I! Send me.'"*

I cannot imagine how hard it would be for Isaiah knowing what was to become of Israel. But his heart was willing. And God used him in mighty ways. He was grieved, but although most rejected God in Israel, there was a remnant who chose to believe. In the latter chapters of the book of Isaiah, he told of Israel not only becoming prosperous in the end times, but also in the millennium. Isaiah had a willing heart. God knows who is willing and He knows who is disobedient. Isaiah warned Israel what would happen if they did not obey. In the long run, God ultimately blessed them.

Sarah and Cosmo also have shown a willing heart, ready to serve in whatever capacity God has for them. Not only were they sent to Asia to minister to people, but God also sent them to Idaho. They use their dojo as a place of intentional sharing of God's love and good news, and not just as a business. They have been diligent to listen for His voice and to follow His direction. They willingly go—sharing God's love with those around them.

*A FRIGHTENED WORLD NEEDS
A FEARLESS CHURCH.
- A.W. TOZER*

CHAPTER 6

Patrick

From Fear to Boldness

HOW DO YOU APPROACH PEOPLE WHO YOU FEEL YOU CANNOT RELATE TO OR ARE DIFFERENT FROM YOU?

Do you shy away? It's a natural human emotion to fear confrontation with someone we don't really feel we know or relate to, whether it's a homeless person or a family member. Once you overcome that fear, you may realize that whatever God has called you to do in this situation may be risky, but it's your assignment, and you don't need to know all the answers. You just need to act boldly. Once you do, you'll find that maybe they really aren't that different and maybe you just perceived them as different.

SOMETIMES, GOD TAKES YOU OUT OF YOUR COMFORT ZONE!

I think the more we see how much God loves everyone without partiality, we can open up our hearts to anyone and everyone.

There are many instances when we may be fearful of reaching out to someone. In today's world, Christians are being persecuted for their faith, or there may be that person at work who always yells at you. I truly believe God honors our steps of faith even if we may be shaking in our shoes.

Patrick is a big burly guy with a huge heart for others. He has been a military chaplain, ministering to hundreds over the past several years. He shares the following example of bold action from early in his ministry. Even though he was nervous and fearful, he followed the spiritual prodding in his heart and purposefully took steps to reach out to people he may never have thought to minister to. He knew God wanted him in that place at that particular time.

Patrick

My senior year at South Dakota State University, I entered a Christian book store to look for interesting reading. I had been in the store only five minutes and the owner of the store put his hand on my shoulder and stated, "You need to come into the prison with me and be involved in a prison ministry." I did not know the kind gentlemen, but his presence was never about himself. It centered around God and ministry to inmates. I do not remember him saying much to me, other than the words shared above.

I entered the Sioux Falls State Penitentiary for orientation to ministry classes held by the correctional chaplain there. He also was kind and did not share much about himself. His words centered around God and the possibilities of new relationships that incarcerated men could have with Christians who would befriend them. And, the goal was to bring inmates to Christ through relationships.

You may ask how I felt about going into the prison. I was nervous about the idea. I was afraid of entering the prison to talk with an inmate. I thought this idea of going into the prison was scary. Nevertheless, I kept entering the prison for the three 1.5 hours orientation classes and liked the presentations. I welcomed the interest the chaplain showed in each of us, and he fluently spoke about ministry to inmates through friendship. I remained nervous and somewhat uncomfortable all the way up to the time when I finally got to meet the inmate I was assigned to.

I had prayed and spoken to Christian friends. They encouraged me to pursue the part-time ministry. The fourth Monday evening when I met my inmate friend, I immediately noticed he had been beaten up recently: bruises on his face, black and blue. He looked as if he had been close to death. I did not wish what he looked like upon anyone. I remained nervous. He told me that the guy across the room took a full soda pop can and placed it in a tube sock and beat him with it. This was interesting. The fella who beat him up was in the same visitation room with all of us. I remained nervous.

However, the turning point for the fear and anxiety to wane happened when I watched the chaplain start handing out cups of milk and cookies to the inmates and we who had gone through orientation. For some reason, I thought of little boys and children eating cookies and dunking them in milk. I felt God's presence and I sensed him saying, "I love these incarcerated men. And, I love you." I also sensed some humor. I was a grown man, physically strong, yet had been afraid, now calmed and humored by seeing smiling faces and cheerful voices indulge for moments in the sweet chocolate chip cookies and cold milk. My taste buds danced. My heart felt God's presence. As I write now, my eyes well up with tears because God can forgive anyone, and He showed me His power that night with the chaplain serving us cookies and milk.

The inmates and we each had something in common: love for chocolate chip cookies and cold milk. We are human. I was carried out of my comfort zone and comforted by God.

God created us and gave us all the desire for healthy relationships. Man to Man Prison Ministry took me out of my comfort zone, and God comforted me after I took steps into that ministry.

I understand Patrick's fear of being in a prison, not knowing what would happen if something went wrong, but the great thing about this testimony is that Patrick discovered that the inmates were just like him. They were each an individual God created and loved. They just needed a little encouragement and direction.

Acts chapter nine tells of the Apostle Paul's conversion. Talk about unpredictable! No one in his inner circle would have predicted this.

Here was a man who was known for persecuting Christians and then encountered the Lord who changed his life forever. But beginning in verse ten, another man, named Ananias, is asked by the Lord to move out of his comfort zone. He is quite nervous about this path the Lord would have him follow.

> *"Now there was a certain disciple at Damascus, named Ananias; and the Lord said to him in a vision, "Ananias." And he said, 'Behold, here am I Lord.' And the Lord said to him, 'Arise and go to the street called Straight, and inquire at the house of Judas for a man from Tarsus named Saul, for behold, he is praying, and he has seen in a vision a man named Ananias come in and lay hands on him, so that he might regain his sight.' But Ananias answered, 'Lord, I have heard from many about this man., about how much harm he did to Thy saints at Jerusalem; and here he has authority from the chief priests to bind all who call upon Thy name.'*
>
> *But the Lord said to him, 'Go, for he is a chosen instrument of Mine, to bear My name before the Gentiles and kings and the sons of Israel; for I will show him how much he must suffer for My name's sake.'*
>
> *And Ananias departed and entered the house, and after laying hands on him said, 'Brother Saul, the Lord Jesus, who appeared to you on the road by which you were coming, has sent me so that you may regain your sight and be filled with the Holy Spirit.' And immediately there fell from his eyes something like scales, and*

he regained his sight, and he arose and was baptized; and he took food and was strengthened."

ACTS 9:10-19

Now we know how extremely powerful Paul's ministry became. God changed his name from Saul to Paul. He had a new life, a new name, and an impactful ministry—and it took the obedience of Ananias to start Paul on his way. Ananias took steps to be bold in his faith. He followed through on a difficult, scary task—going to meet Paul, the persecutor of believers. Ananias did what the Lord had for him to do, even though he was fearful. We have many examples of Paul's life, but we only have this one about Ananias: he was uncertain, he was rightfully afraid, and he was anxious about what God wanted him to do—but he took steps to be bold in his faith. Because Ananias was bold, Paul was able to begin his journey of sharing God's grace with others.

Because Patrick was bold and overcame his initial fear, he saw that the men in prison loved chocolate chip cookies. They could still enjoy something while in prison. He saw the inmates as people the same as you or me. I am sure all these years later that he can see those he ministers to in his current ministry through those same eyes: Eyes of compassion. I want that kind of bold faith: To not be fearful and to continually move forward on the narrow path God has me following.

GOD IS GOD. BECAUSE HE IS GOD, HE IS WORTHY OF MY TRUST AND OBEDIENCE. I WILL FIND REST NOWHERE BUT IN HIS HOLY WILL THAT IS UNSPEAKABLY BEYOND MY LARGEST NOTIONS OF WHAT HE IS UP TO.
– ELISABETH ELLIOT

CHAPTER 7

Melissa

Tenacity of Faith

As mothers, we are given a mission field right in our own home, raising our children to love the Lord and then learning to leave them completely in the Lord's hands. Sometimes, this is hard. Melissa has her mission field in Africa with the people there, *and* she has her children. When I heard her speak at our missions conference, I was inspired by how she has learned to do both with a heart for the Lord.

Stepping out in faith doesn't always look exciting and dramatic. Sometimes it is a quiet matter, blossoming out of some delicate, inexplicable hope that whispers gently, "just trust Me". In the story of the infant Moses' miraculous deliverance from the death edict pronounced by Pharoah on all Hebrew male babies, the undeniable thrill of Moses' perilous basket ride down the river and his rescue by a noble daughter of the very house of the one who called for his death captures our attention – and rightly so, as it is a glorious display of God's divine will and providence. But, as I've grown into my own God-given role as a missionary to West Africa and mother to eight, the tenacity of the faith of Moses' mother has stood out to me in ever-increasing significance.

One of the most remarkable things about Moses' mother's role in this story is not what we do read about her, but what we don't – that is, we are not told her name. As the narrative of Exodus unfolds, of course, we do eventually learn her name, Jochebed, but at the moment of her most stunning display of courageous faith, she remains simply "mother". Oh, how this resonates to my mother's heart! In northern Togo, where my family and I serve, all women with children are called "Maman." As we arrived on the field, it was startling to be referred to by other adults not by my first name, or even Mrs. Fife, but just as one more Maman in a city populated by thousands of Mamans. This was the beginning of God's work in my own heart to expose the idols that I had petted and polished as diligently as if they were made of precious metal and stone. My idols, like most Westerners, don't look like the physical idols of my animist Togolese neighbors, however they are just as real and just as destructive of my relationship to the Only True God.

Even as my husband and I answered God's call to overseas missions later in life, after 18 years of marriage and already seven children in, I was convinced that life on a foreign field was something that I could accomplish through my own industry and faithfulness. But within weeks of arriving in our new, impossibly hot and humid home, woken up by 4 a.m. Muslim prayer call every morning, separated by three continents and an ocean from my firstborn, a sophomore in college at the time, disconcerted—to put it mildly—by the thought of ants and even roaches freely roaming the house after the lights were out as if it was their personal nightclub, God broke wide open the pretenses of my self-reliance, shattering every expectation of life as a missionary mother and wife. Not only were my own efforts woefully inadequate, my heart was shamefully exposed—a heart consumed by a desire to worship at the altars of security and self-Importance.

As I learned to survive in a world so very beautiful but so very different from the one I'd known for all thirty-nine years of my life, God used the time of my first year on the field to tear me down, so He could remold me into what He had purposed me for, before the very foundations of the earth had even been created. He wanted for me, He wants for all of us a Jochebed faith—a faith so unshakeable, as deep as the dark, still parts of the ocean depths, as all-encompassing as a heavy blanket of winter snow that I had grown up with as a girl in northern Wisconsin and missed dreadfully during my dry and sandy first Christmas in Africa. A Jochebed faith is a mother's faith. It is so often still and is found not necessarily in the actions taken, but in a heart surrendered. A heart that doesn't know what will come, especially when the path God's leading you down looks like it leads off a cliff.

Certainly, Jochebed must have felt the incredible weight of surrendering her tiny child to a mighty, rushing river protected by nothing but a water-proof woven basket. For most of us, our challenges will not look as dramatic as Jochebed's and yet, they are still there. Even the mundanity of daily life, especially as a mother, whether in Idaho or Togo, can speak its serpentine doubt into our souls, causing us to question if we can trust the promises of God. It is in those moments, both grandiose and subtle, that our faith becomes not something amorphous and distant, but the guiding beacon by which we orient everything in us and about us. Faith becomes not something we do or have, but something as vital and life-sustaining as the beating of our own heart. And I pray that my heart – and yours - continues to beat with the same devotion and trust that inspired Jochebed to lay her precious son, not just in a woven basket, but at the very feet of God. For the God who has promised is faithful and sovereign, and He calls each one of us to surrender every hope and dream to Him, through the divine gift of His marvelous grace. Do the hard things, take bold steps, surrender that which your heart holds dearest! Not all are called to be a Deborah, or a Ruth, or a Mary – but all of us are called to be a Jochebed, women of tenacious and abiding faith.

Melissa, although not expecting life to evolve this way, fully embraces what God has for her and surrenders her heart to trust Him. She moves forward on the path God has laid out for her family and trusts God in each step. Like Jochebed, her faith is tenacious. What about you? God will give you clarity on where and whom to serve as you trust the promises of God.

IT IS NOT MY ABILITY, BUT MY RESPONSE TO GOD'S ABILITY THAT COUNTS.
– CORRIE TEN BOOM

CHAPTER 8

Jane's Grandparents

The Heart Of A Caregiver

Everyone has a unique calling from God, and it always seems as if it is tailor-made to your gifts and the desires of your heart. I greatly admire those who minister to anyone with special needs, even those who take care of an elderly parent or a chronically ill child. True compassion shines love with such brilliance. It can be exhausting and extend the caregiver to their fullest. It may keep them up at night or cause them to feel completely overwhelmed. But they are carrying out God's plan of love and redemption. I am thankful for this example of Christ's love that we can share.

" 'But Mephibosheth, your Master's grandson, will eat here at my table'…And from that time on, Mephibosheth ate regularly at David's table, like one of the

King's own sons...And Mephibosheth, who was crip-
pled in both feet lived in Jerusalem and ate regularly
at the King's table."

II Samuel 9

Mephibosheth was King Saul's grandson, Jonathon's
son. Both his father and grandfather were gone, dead after
the political transition from Saul to David. The relationship between David and Saul was complicated: Jonathan
and he had been boyhood friends, yet Saul had attempt-
ed to assassinate him! Saul was violent, tortured, possibly
mentally ill, charming, a leader, a failure, and an enemy,
but still loved.

Jane is the daughter of another complicated figure: a
teenage father, a homeless runaway, a castaway child, an
addict, violent, tortured, mentally ill, and a murderer, but
still loved.

Mephibosheth was powerless over his situation. He
was at the mercy of King David's regime. As an heir to
the former king, he had no standing, and was actually in
danger. He should have been cast away, put to death as
other heirs had been.

Jane was at the mercy of the state, a four-month-old
in a ramshackle old home in the worst part of the city
with an addict mother, a father in prison sentenced to
thirty years, and strangers shooting guns in the house,

burning her with cigarettes. She was a castaway, disposable, and neglected.

Mephibosheth was crippled in both feet, disabled as a result of a mistake someone else made, a life changed by a horrible accident that he had to live with the painful consequences of for the rest of his life. He was most likely looked down upon, probably needed help with basic tasks, depressed, hopeless, ignored, and marginalized, though the God of the universe had a plan.

Jane was born with a genetic anomaly close to autism that was no fault of her own, a life changed by the way DNA formed at conception. She has the painful consequences of a lifetime of disability. She has been shunned by neighbors, asked not to come back to kindergarten, and not invited to play or attend birthday parties. She needed help with basic needs, a child with high anxiety and no way to handle it, ignored, and marginalized. But the God of the universe has a plan.

Mephibosheth was redeemed. King David broke protocol and convention. He changed the rules because of love. He restored ties and granted integrity and purpose. Mephibosheth was treated like one of David's own sons.

Jane was redeemed. Her grandparents looked past the lifelong commitment of taking care of a special needs child. When it would have been easier to say, "it's not my job," they chose to love her and her mother in the midst of the pain and chaos. Opportunities were fought for. Rights in education and respect were earned. Tears, hard choices, and sleepless nights in prayer led to her being adopted by her grandparents and by the King of Kings.

All of us are broken because of sin, because of other's actions, and because of our own choices. But the God of the universe has a plan. Redemption.

King David broke protocol and convention by allowing Mephibosheth to join them for meals. His heart was compassionate. He provided for Mephibosheth, and he set an example for everyone to follow. He did not need to do that, but he knew it would mean everything to Mephibosheth and it would be an example of love and compassion to everyone there.

This couple loves their granddaughter so much. They took the responsibility for Jane to give her a better life, and fought for this opportunity to take care of her. Jane has been prayed over for many hours. They were following God's direction and were instrumental in God's plan of redemption for Jane's life. What a great example for all of us.

*This is a warm and compassionate story full of love. I want to let you know that the names and details were changed to protect privacy.

YOU WERE MADE BY GOD AND FOR
GOD, AND UNTIL YOU UNDERSTAND
THAT, LIFE WILL NEVER MAKE SENSE.
- RICK WARREN

CHAPTER 9

Rick

The Turning Point

MIRACLES CAN OCCUR

IN THE SMALLEST OF TOWNS,

MOMENTS, AND STORIES.

WE ALL HAVE A STORY TO TELL

WHEN WE LIVE BOLDLY FOR CHRIST,

AND WE CAN MAKE AN IMPACT

IN THE LIVES OF OTHERS.

I kept hearing about this pastor from a little church out in a small town here in Idaho where I live. I heard how he was always meeting with people and mentoring them. I also heard how the most important thing to him was that he wanted to share the gospel with as many people as possible so they may live in Heaven for eternity. I knew I needed to invite this man to share his story. You see, he invested in my son-in-law's life for a long time, and I believe it was a great encouragement to my son-in-law's parched soul.

This is a man, not from a populated place or huge church or enormous ministry, but a man who is meeting the needs of local people who need guidance in a small town in Idaho. Some people grow and learn to love the Lord over time, but for some, it's a complete turn: A pivotal moment in time where they make the decision to follow Christ and be bold in their life for Him. Pastor Rick is one of those people. God met him directly in that moment in his life, and that's when Rick made the decision to follow and serve him. That decision has allowed Rick to be bold and purposeful in his life and ministry.

Pastor Rick

"For I fully expect and hope that I will never be ashamed, but that I will continue to be bold for Christ, as I have been in the past. And I trust that my life will bring honor to Christ, whether I live or die."

PHILIPPIANS 1:20 NLT

When I was asked to share my experience of being bold for Jesus, I was quite honored and humbled by the way my friends Shane and Jessica approached and asked me if I would consider doing it. I heard the Lord speaking through them to me, so I knew better than to say no. We had just finished with Sunday morning Service when Shane asked me if he and Jessica could speak with me for a few minutes. As I completed the normal discussions with different ones from my flock and came up to them, I heard the Lord tell me "yes you can". I've learned over the years to not argue when He tells me something, but to just be obedient and say yes. Running from and arguing with Jesus does not work!

To fully explain how I came about being as bold as I am, I have to go back in time to April of 1994. Everything changed in me when I came face to face with Jesus during the very first Promise Keepers event that took place at the Boise Hawks Stadium in Boise. My mother-in-law had purchased tickets for my father-in-law, a brother-in-law, and I to go to the men's event. Unfortunately at the time I was thinking as I drove all of the way up to Boise from Caldwell, how I would rather be going fishing, hunting, riding my 4-wheeler or anything else than going to some men's conference with my in-laws. I mean I was really mad about it! When I arrived, I went in and began looking for my in-laws but couldn't find them. It was while I was look-ing for them that I heard someone call out "Rick, Rick, up here." So I turned to find a few of the men that I attended church with calling and waving at me to come over and sit with them. I thought to myself at that point that this could really be advantageous for me. If I said I couldn't find my in-laws, which was true, then I could stay for a little while and then sneak out after an hour or so and no one would really ever notice. That's what I thought. Little did I know that the Lord had something very dif-ferent in store for me. The conference began with prayer of course, and then the first speaker was introduced to the some five thousand men attending the event. We were sitting in some bleachers some distance away from the stage when the speaker began talking about playing games with God, you know, being saved but not really being committed. When he was finished speaking, he invited any of us men to come down and pray if we were sick of playing the game with God and really desired to walk with Jesus.

To this day, I do not know how I got down to that stage. All I knew was I was standing in front of the stage looking up. Then, all of sudden I wasn't looking at men, a stage, or anything found on earth. When my focus became clear I was looking right into the most beautiful set of eyes I had ever seen in my whole life! I was looking at Jesus. I knew Him instantly and as He wrapped His arms around me, I knew that I was loved dearly. I do not know how long I was there with Him, but it seemed like quite a while. He told me that I wasn't going to play games any longer and that I was now His servant and that He had a great ministry ahead of me to accomplish. But He also said that He would be with me from that time on. When He told me it was time to return, I asked "do I have to?" and He smiled warmly at me and said yes but not to forget that He is with me always. Then He reached out to me and put a physical mark on me that remains to this day. When I arrived (for lack of better terms) I was again in front of that stage and the coach who had asked us if we were tired of playing games and to come forward was looking down at me. I was the only one left standing there. He asked me if I had just been with Jesus and all I could do was shake my head yes through tears of happiness. They brought me up on stage and all of the men there laid hands on me and prayed for the ministries the Lord was going to do through me.

Since that time, the Lord has given me the opportunity to become an elder in a Baptist church, a teacher of the Word which His Spirit has poured into me, a Pastor, as well as a church planter. God has given me a boldness that I could not have without Him. Because of this I have been purposeful in reaching out to my small community. I have learned to go out of my way to serve and reach those around me. No matter how rough around the edges they seem. I have learned to love these people unconditionally. None of which I could have or possibly would have done on my own. I have walked with the Lord by the power of His Spirit ever since!

There are many other things that have taken place in my life since then. All of which were not humanly possible. But with God all things are possible. There is one thing I've learned through all of this; and that is that when you are walking by the power of the Holy Spirit, you can totally trust Him and you can approach His throne with boldness and confidence.

There are countless mentions of Moses in Scripture. He wrote the law God instructed him to give the Israelites. He wrote the Pentateuch, which are the first five books in our Bible. His life is divided into three sections of forty years each. The first forty years, he grows up and lives in Egypt being raised in Pharaoh's court. The second part of his life, Moses became a shepherd and spent his days out in the solitude of the wilderness with his sheep. In Exodus chapter three, he has what you would call a life-altering experience, and it becomes a pivotal turning point in Moses's life. Not only for his life, but for Israel's future.

So Moses is out with his sheep and sees something in the distance. It catches his attention and he goes to investigate. He is drawn to a bush, as it appears to be on fire and it is not consuming the bush. Exodus 3:2-3 explains,

> *"And the angel of the Lord appeared to him in a flame of fire in the midst of the bush. So he looked and behold, the bush was burning with fire but the bush was not consumed. Then Moses said, 'I will now turn aside and see this great sight.'*

MOSES HIDES HIS FACE
OUT OF REVERENT FEAR OF GOD.

Moses has been sad for his people who have been enslaved in Egypt, and God shares His grief and concern in verses 7-10.

> *"And the Lord said: 'I have surely seen the oppression of My people who are in Egypt, and have heard their cry because of their taskmasters, for I know their sorrows. For I have come down to deliver them out of the hand of the Egyptians, and to bring them up from that land, to a land flowing with milk and honey, to the place of the Canaanites, and the Hittites and the Amorites, and the Perizzites and the Hivites and the Jebusites. Now therefore, behold, the cry of the children of Israel has come to me and I have also seen the oppression with which the Egyptians oppress them.*

Come now, therefore, and I will send you to Pharaoh, that you may bring My people, the children of Israel out of Egypt. "

God knew of the terrible situation. He would send Moses as an ambassador to represent Him and address Pharaoh. Moses's first reaction is like most of ours would be. Uh what? I am not able to do that. So he tells God and God responds in the following verses,

"But Moses said to God, 'Who am I that I should go to Pharaoh, and that I should bring the children of Israel out of Egypt?' So He (God) said, I will certainly be with you. And this shall be a sign to you that I have sent you: When you have brought the people out of Egypt, you shall serve God on this mountain. "

Moses did not feel qualified and he did not feel able, but God assured him. God promised him that He would deliver Israel out of bondage. God gave Moses a purpose, a ministry, and a boldness to go where Moses did not want to go and do things Moses did not feel capable of doing. Many things transpire before the Israelites can leave Egypt, but just as He promised, they are able to leave, led by Moses.

We are often fearful. Maybe our heart is pounding to talk with a person or to take a step to help someone. We may even be fearful of what will happen if we do obey. We need to take that step. Pastor Rick was sitting in that stadium knowing in his heart he must move his feet and take a stand. Like Moses, God let Rick know that he was chosen for ministry and that He would be with him. That He would equip him to do what He needed him to do. The men's event was Rick's "burning bush" experience. It was the pivotal event that changed the direction of his life and gave him his life's purpose.

It has not been easy. Pastor Rick has supported himself when the church could not. He has, day in and day out, given of himself and his own resources to the people of this small town. But God will bless him for his faithfulness, for God chose him for this work. Has God chosen you too?

THIS IS WHAT THE PAST IS FOR! EVERY EXPERIENCE GOD GIVES US. EVERY PERSON HE PUTS IN OUR LIVES IS THE PERFECT PREPARATION FOR THE FUTURE THAT ONLY HE CAN SEE.
- CORRIE TEN BOOM

CHAPTER 10

John and Joanne

Taking The Next Step

Our paths in life often take us in directions we least expect. Or perhaps we have to wait and wait to move forward on a project that clearly seemed like it was the best choice, and it's confusing as to why! But waiting is sometimes the best thing to do. When you think of being purposeful or intentional, it makes you think of moving forward and taking action now! Yet I believe sometimes God takes us on a slower path to grow and learn. In the waiting, you are gaining patience during the waiting phase itself, which causes growth and will only help with future ministry and life experiences. He has a perfect plan that He may not be ready to implement, or the time has not yet come for it to be revealed. Be still. God's got the rest of it all worked out.

I also think our life can have a totally different look. I think of Ruth and Boaz. They did not anticipate any of the events that occurred, but in this beloved and exquisite story of only four chapters lies an important story which links Ruth to the line of Jesus. As many of you know, Ruth and her sister-in-law and mother-in-law all lose their husbands. Ruth's mother-in-law, Naomi, tells her daughters-in-law to go home to their own people. Ruth begs to stay with Naomi. Here we have the famous passage in 1:16,

> *But Ruth said, Do not urge me to leave you or turn back from following you; for where you go, I will go, and where you lodge, I will lodge. Your people shall be my people and your God, my God."*

Clearly this was not a known plan ahead of time for Ruth or Naomi. But plans change, circumstances change. And we follow accordingly. Later Ruth gleans in Boaz's fields. Boaz takes notice of her and learns of her plight. He makes arrangements for her to be able to glean extra for Naomi, and Naomi starts seeing God's lovingkindness and mercy because of Ruth.

Ruth and Boaz continue their story and end up marrying and having a son—a son who is an ancestor of Jesus. Ruth's path changed from being a childless widow to becoming part of the lineage of Christ. History is made and changed forever. We also make history in what we do with our lives. We can go through each day concentrating on our home, family, ministry, or work. I appreciate those who, although the path may not be what they intended, continue on, and then the way becomes clear.

The following story is from a family in our church who has faithfully served in many capacities, and now a new path has become clear for their lives.

Joanne and John

In so many ways, our steps towards ministry resemble ordinary life. As in any decisions regular people make, we look at our skill sets, our desires and dreams, we ask respected counselors for advice, and we set out on the path one step at a time. We had no idea how God would reveal a call toward missions, but with prayer and some faith, we knew we could take the first step and see what happened.

God formed my, Joanne's, desire and dreams for missions at a young age. I grew up in a family that fully engaged in supporting missionaries. This passion for missions took root in me as a young child, and as I grew in my faith, I continued to have a desire towards ministry. I was able to go on several mission trips during my college years. After college, I took a job as a secondary English teacher at a Christian school in Guam.

While I was ready and willing to serve in missions from childhood, John's path took longer. Although he was saved at age nine, it wasn't until his first years serving in the Air Force in Guam that he began to grow in faith. Godly men close to him modeled what it looked like to live with daily faith, and his own relationship with God began to gain depth.

It seems ironic now, but part of my decision to date John involved letting go of my narrow idea of "marrying into ministry." Here was a man who loved God and served others, but not only was he not currently in missions or ministry, he appeared to have no plans or passions toward that path. Yet, with solid counsel, prayer, and faith to let go of my preconceived ideas, our relationship moved forward. We were married in 2009. In those years, God brought more and more opportunities for John to use his mechanical skills to help others. He was able to go on three service mission trips to Yap, Micronesia. These opportunities used his skills and fueled a godly passion to serve. During our six years in Guam, God was developing John's spiritual person and implanting in us dreams and desires we didn't quite realize we had until we had to leave our home in the Pacific tropics. In 2013, we were transferred to the high desert of Mountain Home, Idaho.

My ministry as a Christian school teacher halted as I found I was expecting, and I switched gears to be a stay-at-home mom. John's ministry opportunities seemed vague, as the need for an honest, skilled mechanic was less urgent. And soon, even his position in the Air Force was no longer a certainty, as dramatic military cutbacks slashed into every rank. What would we do if we could do anything we wanted? We were forced to consider this.

Then, one Good Friday, on a hike with friends, the idea of missionary aviation was suggested. John could easily visualize being a pilot-mechanic to serve remote locations. Our trips to Micronesia had shown us how basic supplies can dramatically help the mission efforts there. However, this was the first time he had considered aviation as the means to help. To me, the possibility was exciting—I had made my decision to go "wherever God called" years ago.

And so we talked to a recruiter. And we took a tour. And we prayed. We met with our pastor and respected mentors. And we took the first step. There were two aspects to our path to ministry occurring simultaneously: active development of skills and qualifications, and intentional faithful ministry where we were. For myself, those next six years involved a lot of embracing motherhood, engaging in Bible studies, and serving in children's ministry, while supporting John's training. These things seemed natural, and normal parts of a life of faith.

Our path included a lot of training for John while he was serving full time in the Air Force.

In a short time but with a great deal of effort, he became a proficient pilot with all necessary certificates. He enjoyed every opportunity to fly to build his hours. Simultaneously, John was digging into his required Bible courses, absorbing God's Word and learning to study at a new level.

With prayer and counsel, and just taking the next step, we continued. John's next step was to become a certified Airframe and Powerplant mechanic. However, we knew we'd be leaving the military a mere six years short of full retirement. God continued to impress upon us to move forward. The next step was to leave active duty, sell our house, our airplane, and move our family to a small apartment in Tulsa, Oklahoma so John could attend AMT school full-time. We took the step.

Despite interruptions of a pandemic, John successfully became a licensed Aircraft Maintenance Technician in July 2020. We returned home to Idaho, where God provided employment which allowed John to gain valuable experience in the mechanic field. He is also sharpening his flying skills by flight instruction. As the final steps of our application process are completed, we look to God to see what opportunities await.

In all these years, we have been mentored by our pastors. We've been encouraged by parents and by countless prayer warriors. And as God has allowed, we have simply taken the next step.

Is God preparing you for something bigger? Has He put you in a waiting period or holding pattern that feels frustrating? Are you willing to take the next step?

That is the key right there. *"And as God has allowed, we have simply taken the next step."* God's path for John and Joanne seemed to change over the years, but He prepared them all along as they took one step at a time. John and Joanne knew they were obeying God's will for them. Sometimes it is not something dramatic or dynamic, but by following the right path, they can just take the next step.

About five years ago, in my late fifties, I decided to write my first book. Such a different path than I had been on! I soon was in over my head, not understanding what I was doing. BUT, I knew it was what I was supposed to do. For years, people had told me that I needed to tell my story. I was not a writer, but I understood how my story might help someone else. And just like Ruth had not even imagined her husband dying, moving to another country, meeting Boaz, and getting remarried, our life can suddenly change. John and Joanne "thought" they knew what they would do with their lives, but they waited, and God opened up a new path for them, even better than they imagined.

We live in a "now" society. We expect things to happen exactly how we think, and when that doesn't happen, we are confused and disgruntled. But there is something great about resting in the moment. Seeing the beauty of today. That doesn't mean we don't intentionally plan, but we need to be willing to change plans.

I admire this young couple for hanging in there and persevering along this path to serve. They are now preparing to serve in a way they may not have imagined fifteen years ago.

THE LIFE OF FAITH IS LIVED ONE DAY AT A TIME. AND IT HAS TO BE LIVED – NOT ALWAYS LOOKED FORWARD TO AS THOUGH THE "REAL" LIVING WERE AROUND THE NEXT CORNER. IT IS TODAY FOR WHICH WE ARE RESPONSIBLE. GOD STILL OWNS TOMORROW.
-ELISABETH ELLIOT

CHAPTER 11

Sandy

Live Outwardly

For the past several years, I have worked in our kids ministry at church on Wednesday nights with a woman named Sandy. We worked with different age groups, and I did not cross paths with her much at first; however, eventually I did, and I spent time getting to know her. I was able to see what a solid young woman she is, and I have also seen how she ministers to everyone around her. This servant attitude is a true gift!

My oldest daughter needed assistance recently after a surgery and Sandy changed her busy schedule to take care of two of my granddaughters for several days. Not because it was convenient, but because it was needed. Her mom also messages me encouraging words every time I write a blog—*the apple doesn't fall far from the tree.* I learned of her neighborhood ministry, and knew her heart was a giving heart. She loves the Lord. I am thankful she was able to share her story.

Sandy

"Remember this: Whoever sows sparingly will also reap sparingly, and whoever sows generously will also reap generously. Each of you should give what you have decided in your heart to give, not reluctantly or under compulsion, for God loves a cheerful giver. And God is able to bless you abundantly, so that in all things at all times, having all that you need, you will abound in every good work. As it is written: 'They have freely scattered their gifts to the poor; their righteousness endures forever.' Now he who supplies seed to the sower and bread for food will also supply and increase your store of seed and will enlarge the harvest of your righteousness. You will be enriched in every way so that you can be generous on every occasion, and through us your generosity will result in thanksgiving to God. This service that you perform is not only supplying the needs of the Lord's people but is also overflowing in many expressions of thanks to God. Because of the service by which you have proved yourselves, others will praise God for the obedience that accompanies your confession of the gospel of Christ, and for your generosity in sharing with them and with everyone else. And in their prayers for you their hearts will go out to you, because of the surpassing grace God has given you. Thanks be to God for his indescribable gift!"

2 CORINTHIANS 9:6-15

It is so easy to focus on ourselves—our needs, our wants, our families, our homes, our church, our friends, our activities. It is easy and comfortable to surround ourselves with like-minded and like-faithed people. And, while those priorities are important, God calls us to something more. To turn ourselves outward—to live outwardly—whoever and wherever we are to bring His love and His light to those around us. Sometimes it may not feel significant or important, but each new friend or act of service is an act of faith and offering to God.

I used to wonder what my spiritual gifts were and felt frustrated because I could not determine what they were. I felt like I was disappointing God by not recognizing and utilizing my spiritual gifts. I was also terrified of talking about God unless I knew the other person was a believer. I felt double-disappointing—I did not know what my spiritual gifts were, and I was scared to talk to people about God. So, I prayed. I prayed God would open my eyes to my gifts and give me the words to speak for Him. He answered those prayers but not how I expected.

He did not open my eyes to my own spiritual gifts. He opened my eyes to the needs around me and convicted me to serve where needed. So, I did. I served where I saw a need. I served at church, I served my friends, as well as my neighbors, my kids' school, and the families of the kids at school. Most of the time I did not feel gifted. I did not feel like I was doing anything important or special, but I knew I was being obedient. The more I served, the more I recognized the needs of others and the more I learned about my ministry preferences. Little acts of service that can seem so insignificant please God, can be fulfilling to us as believers and make a great difference in the lives of those we are serving. I started pouring myself into the lives of a variety of people, and God was using that to establish close relationships with believers and non-believers alike—allowing me to serve them and allowing me to be someone they could count on and trust.

Concurrently, I was still stuck and struggling with talking about God and not wanting to risk these new, fragile relationships. Then God started to change my mindset about that, too. Rather than waiting for the perfect opportunity and the right words (which rarely came or, if they did, I seldom had the courage to take advantage of them) God showed me I could talk about it like I would any other friend or hobby. People love to talk about their interests and talking about Him in that context made it seem easier, light-hearted, and more natural. It took a little practice, but that was the ticket for me. I started talking about God like I would any other friend and about church activities like any other activity. If nothing else, it lets people know quickly that I'm a believer. But it also opens the door to conversations and invitations either in that moment or in the future. Some of the people I least expect to already be Christians already are. Some people I think would never want to talk about God do desire further conversation. Some people clearly have no interest in discussing further, but God still plants the seed, no matter how small. What surprises me the most about this tactic is that no one ever seems offended or avoids me afterwards. It gives me a tiny glimpse into other people's views on God and a starting point going forward.

God is now showing me that our service to Him is constant and yet also ever-changing. As we grow and our life circumstances change, so do our opportunities. With young children at home, it might make sense to bring neighborhood kids along to a church's kids' program but that might not be where God works if the children at home are older or if there are no children at home. God may provide an opportunity to start an at-home Bible Study with other women who are interested in learning more about God but may not feel comfortable going to a church-affiliated Bible Study. But as life and work change, focus and time might be directed elsewhere, and that opportunity might also fade. Just because a service opportunity is present in one phase of life does not mean it will be in another and that's okay. It is not an indication of failure—it just means that God is working elsewhere for the time-being. There will always be opportunities to serve, to share God's love, to shine our light for Him and to live outwardly.

Yes! There will always be opportunities to serve. Paul tells us in 2 Timothy to avoid things that are useless, but keep active in the things that count. 2 Timothy 15-16 says,

> *"Be diligent to present yourself approved to God as a workman who does not need to be ashamed, handling accurately the word of truth. But avoid*

THIS GENERATION HAS FORGOTTEN THAT THE GOSPEL MESSAGE DOES NOT CLEAN UP AND SHINE THE OUTSIDE OF A PERSON. RATHER IT BORES INTO THE VERY HEART AND SOUL OF A PERSON AND RADICALLY CHANGES THAT PERSON FROM THE INSIDE FOREVER.

– A.W. TOZER

CHAPTER 12

Rebekah

Getting Out Of Your Comfort Zone

You can search the world over,

but some of the best humans you'll meet

will be right in your backyard

where God has placed them.

This next testimony is from a young woman who has been in ministry in our church for twenty-five years. Her husband was our youth pastor, and is now our senior pastor. They were both intricately involved with our kids when they were in the youth ministry. Rebekah spent many hours mentoring and encouraging my three girls, and now she is an amazing pastor's wife. She set up a discipleship team for our young ladies at church, and was faithful to check in on them. She has planned many a mission's trip, and did all the behind-the-scenes work of organizing and planning without ever expecting a thank you. She has set an excellent example for the young girls and women in our church and around the valley.

Rebekah is unassuming and humble and very sweet and respectful. She is also bold for the gospel. She was actually the second person I thought of when choosing people for this book, yet she was one of the last to get her narrative to me. She felt unworthy to be involved with this project because she was not sure if it would seem like she was bragging, once again showing her heart for others and not focusing on herself. I reassured her that others needed to be encouraged in their faith and that God uses our stories to help others.

Rebekah

I love how God directs our steps and brings us into relationships where we can share His love. There have been many times in my life when I felt "in over my head" in a ministry setting. When I am in situations where I feel overwhelmed, I remember God has brought me to this place and He is with me. Second Corinthians 12:9-10

"But he said to me, 'My grace is sufficient for you, for my power is made perfect in weakness.' Therefore I will boast all the more gladly of my weaknesses, so that the power of Christ may rest upon me. For the sake of Christ, then I am content with weaknesses, insults, hardships, persecutions, and calamities. For when I am weak, then I am strong."

Many years ago when I was a college student, I lived in downtown Chicago. All students were given a ministry with which to be involved. I was assigned a ministry in the nearby inner city projects. I met and loved working with kids in that community, and continued in it for my four years at college.

One special memory from that time was attending a retreat out of the city with some of the kids. A few of them had never been to a lakeside camp in the country. It was fun to experience God's creation with them. It was especially fun to hear their thoughts on how dark and how quiet it was outside of the city. Who would have guessed that kids who faced gangs and regular violence would be scared of the dark and the absence of car alarms?

I grew up in the rural Midwest, yet here I was in the middle of a big city. God gave me a place to serve and share his love with children who were very different from me, yet the same as me in so many ways. This was a time of growth and I still enjoy contact with some of those "kids."

Another time of unique relationships was when our kids were in elementary school. I would volunteer at their schools as I was able. God allowed me to have many relationships with other mothers from our neighborhood. I was able to share my faith in a variety of ways.

One memory was talking to a mom about the phrase "Good Samaritan". She was not aware of the story from the Bible and didn't know the history behind this phrase. It was so fun to share how Jesus used this story to teach how to be a good neighbor by caring for all people who cross our path. How wonderful that it carries the same meaning today even for those who don't read the Bible.

> This was a time when God was directing my steps into relationships where I could share about his love. I frequently felt "out of my comfort zone" as I interacted with others whose lives were so different from mine, yet similar in so many ways.

There are many places and people that we may feel uncomfortable around. Maybe we don't consider it a safe situation, dangerous, or even just something that makes us uncomfortable. One thing that would make me uncomfortable would be being around lepers. I know it is much different today, but back in the first century, these people were outcasts from society. No one wanted to be around them. Actually, that was true until the last fifty years even.

Leprosy, several thousand years ago, was believed to be a punishment for sin and a divine curse because it was a chronic and incurable disease until modern times.

In Bible times, lepers lived outside their community and were declared "unclean." They had open sores and covered the bottom part of their face to hide the deformities caused by the disease.

> *"And a leper came to Him, beseeching Him and falling on his knees before Him, and saying to Him, 'If You are willing you can make me clean.' And moved with compassion, He stretched out His hand, and touched him, And said to him, 'I am willing; be cleansed.' And immediately the leprosy left him and he was cleansed. And He sternly warned him and sent him away, and He said to him, 'See that you say nothing to anyone; but go, show yourself to the priest and offer for your cleansing what Moses commanded, for a*

testimony to them.' But he went out and began to proclaim it freely and to spread the news about, to such an extent that Jesus could no longer publicly enter the city, but stayed out in unpopulated areas; and they were coming to Him from everywhere."

MARK 1:40-45

Most people cringed at the mention of leprosy and did not want to be associated with someone with the dreaded disease. However, Jesus had compassion on the leper. Compassion is defined as, "sympathetic pity or concern for the sufferings or misfortunes of others."

The past year with COVID encompassing our lives, the heroes were the nurses. They fought an everyday battle. My sister is a nurse and truly has a heart of compassion. I remember her telling me how hard it was at the hospital when a doctor told them to go attend to a person dying of COVID-19. And they did that for months and months.

Rebekah is not a nurse, but she is that sort of person. She would help someone, no matter the situation. She would not hesitate.

Many years ago, one of her friends from college came to speak at our church. They had gone to school in Chicago at a Christian college. He said Rebekah was a fearless person going into the projects among some dangerous people. She wanted to share the gospel with everyone, no matter the risk.

WHAT ABOUT YOU?

WHERE DO YOU FEEL GOD

LEADING YOU BOLDLY?

LIFT UP YOUR EYES. THE HEAVENLY FATHER WANTS TO BLESS YOU - IN INCONCEIVABLE WAYS TO MAKE YOUR LIFE WHAT YOU NEVER DREAMED IT COULD BE.
- ANNE ORTLUND

CHAPTER 13

Megan

Change of Plans

A re you the type to jump into a group of strangers, or to sit back and wait to be involved? It can be challenging to act boldly if you're an introvert and unsure how to connect with others, but just know that God will use your personality style and gifts to reach who He wants you to reach. Do your part by keeping an open mind!

Thirty years ago when we moved to Boise, we had a weekly swim day up at a beach by the reservoir near our town. I had three little kids at the time and loved going each week. Being new to town, I did not really know those ladies and kids, but was trying to connect with them. I remember one week someone saying, "Look at little Megan with her bright red hair and her mom who looks like a kid herself." The next few years, I did not spend much time with Megan, but as she started growing up, I noticed how determined she was and how she desired to be involved and included in everything. I envied that a little, as I have a hard time joining in when I am unsure of myself.

As she became a young lady, she joined all sorts of activities, and once again, I saw that she did everything with gusto. She was on the worship team, our men's fantasy football league, the softball team, and was a counselor at our church camp in the mountains. She was great with kids, and soon went to college and got her teaching degree. She continued being involved with many activities, and I watched that confidence mature. I was not surprised to see her go to the mission field. She is a strong individual and BOLD in her approach to life. This story will encourage you to overcome disappointment and difficulties, embrace a change of plans and live boldly for God.

Megan

As a little girl I played house a lot. I played it with Barbie dolls and Cabbage Patch dolls. I could even turn a Lego pirate ship battle into some form of house while playing with my younger brother. The idea of being a wife and a mom came naturally to me, and I thought that for sure my life's path would guide me that direction. Fast forward to my late twenties and I was quickly discovering that the ambition of getting married and having a family was not happening. This led to discontentment and anger towards God. I was following Him and serving Him; and yet what I wanted for my life was not being fulfilled. I had also accomplished many of the other things that you tend to check off in your twenties. I had my bachelor's degree in elementary education, a successful career in teaching and coaching, owned a home and a car, and was waiting for the next item to check off. In my mind, that was marriage and having a family of my own. What I wanted for my life was clearly not what God wanted for me.

As I worked through my anger and struggles (for me that was talking and crying about it a lot), I found myself in a new place of contentment and peace with what God had planned for me. I had grown in my singleness and found joy in the path God had given me. It was then that the idea of teaching in Togo, West Africa, was planted in my mind and heart. It took a year for the idea to grow enough for me to take action. What's two years of my life to teach somewhere like West Africa? I could handle that. Or so I thought.

Mango, Togo, West Africa, is sub-Saharan hot and truly in the middle of nowhere. There is a beautiful mission hospital, Hospital of Hope, and many families who serve there. I went to teach the children of those families. Two months into my two-year commitment, I was ready to leave on a plane and not look back. I felt like a failure. I had answered the call God placed on my heart, but now I couldn't finish the commitment. It was too much. Moving to Mango was my first time living anywhere but Idaho. I had left my family, friendships of twenty-five years, my church family, and every comfort I had ever known. I had moved to a place where the language was different, the food was different, the people were different, and the weather was different (have I mentioned how hot it is?). Even the bugs and the teaching were different. There was so much to adjust to that I was overwhelmed by it all. Two years felt like a lifetime and it seemed easier to pack my bags and go home. However, through many tears, lots of prayer, the grace of God, and a lot of patience on my teammates' part, I finished my two years. It became easier to live and serve there and I knew I had fulfilled what God wanted me to do. I left Togo thinking that my work was done and that it would be a good place to visit during my summer breaks in future years. I came home to Idaho determined to start life there again by teaching, coaching, and serving.

I was only weeks back from Togo when an uneasiness settled in me. I couldn't shake it and began to wonder if Idaho was where I was really supposed to be. After many conversations with trusted mentors (and let's be honest, more tears), I began the process to return to Togo for a longer commitment of teaching and serving. I would be lying if I said that I never struggle with the idea of being single - committing to Togo felt like nailing the coffin of marriage shut. But, I serve a God that is faithful in His love, grace, and mercy to me. I am comforted by the call He has placed in my life and rest in knowing that He desires good for me and that I can bring glory to Him through my service to Him. As a little girl, I didn't play school in a setting of Africa, but God has directed my steps to do just that.

With Megan doing everything with such boldness, I can't help but think of Peter. If there was a disciple who was bold and impetuous, it was Peter. He wanted to follow Jesus, but sometimes things didn't always work out "perfectly."

After the feeding of the five thousand, the disciples got into their boat on the Sea of Galilee while Jesus sent the crowds away. But it was getting very stormy, and the boat was getting battered by the waves.

> "And in the fourth watch of the night He came to them, walking on the sea. And when the disciples saw Him walking on the sea, they were frightened, saying, 'It is a ghost!' And they cried out for fear. But immediately Jesus spoke to them, saying, 'Take courage, it is I; do not be afraid.' And Peter answered Him and said, 'Lord, if it is You, command me to come to You on the water.' And He said, 'Come!' And Peter got out of the boat, and walked on the water and came toward Jesus. But seeing the wind, he became afraid, and beginning to sink, he cried out saying, 'Lord, save me!' And immediately Jesus stretched out His hand and took hold of him, and said to him, 'O you of little faith, why did you doubt?' And when they got into the boat, the wind stopped. and those who were in the boat worshipped Him, saying, 'You are certainly God's Son!'

MATTHEW 14:25-33

Peter was a true leader. He was always the first to step in to do something. He stepped out onto the water, but the wind and waves caused him to fear, and he began to sink. His expectations of an easy stroll to meet Jesus were changed by his circumstances. Until Jesus intervened. Peter had good intentions and God knew this because Jesus said He would use Peter to build the church. He knew Peter would mature and He knew He could count on him.

Megan was not sure for several years how God would use her. She made plans for a certain type of life, but anger and struggles (like wind and waves) brought her down until God intervened and directed her to Togo. He is using her to teach children in 120-degree weather with snakes and spiders and things most of us would not be comfortable with.

ARE YOU WILLING TO ACCEPT

A CHANGE OF PLANS FROM GOD?

Purpose: 1. the reason for which something
is done or created
or for which something exists

2. have as one's intention
or objective

"If serving the Lord seems undesirable to you,
then choose for yourselves this day whom you will serve,
whether the gods your ancestors served
beyond the Euphrates, or the gods of the Amorites,
in whose land you are living.
But as for me and my household,
we will serve the Lord."

JOSHUA 24:15

BOLD & BEYOND

PHOTO BY A.J. HOWARD

I LOOK ON FOREIGN MISSIONARIES AS THE SCAFFOLDING ROUND A RISING BUILDING. THE SOONER IT CAN BE DISPENSED WITH THE BETTER – OR RATHER. THE SOONER IT CAN BE TRANSFERRED TO OTHER PLACES TO SERVE THE SAME TEMPORARY PURPOSE.
– HUDSON TAYLOR

CHAPTER 14

Hudson Taylor

Radical Faith

Hudson Taylor was a British Protestant Christian missionary to China and founder of the China Inland Mission. He began his ministry when he was twenty-one. His parents had great influence over their son, as they wanted him to go to the mission field one day and prayed for him to go to China. He spent several years in preparation. He spent much time praying and studying his Bible. He also studied the Mandarin language so he could better communicate with the people in their own language.

Hudson was a radical for his time. He wanted to get to know the Chinese and let them know that he wanted to know their ways rather than trying to force them to be like him. So he decided he would dress like them, and he even grew a long pigtail like they did. He also took Bibles and tracts to give people. He had begun his ministry as part of the Chinese Evangelization Society, but he decided to leave in 1857 and became an independent missionary, knowing God would meet his needs.

He married Maria Dyer, the daughter of a missionary in China. He became ill in 1861, and although his little church in Ningpo had grown, he was forced to move back to England. In England, he worked on translating the Bible into Chinese. He decided that the interior of China needed people who would go and share the gospel. He found that the people in England didn't really care about China. So he made a plan.

He decided to recruit twenty-four missionaries. Two for each of the eleven unreached inland provinces and two for Mongolia. It was a big plan. Greater than most missionaries at the time thought possible. He began to question how he could, in good conscience, send people into an unknown area—their lives and safety were at stake and yet he felt passionate about sharing his faith with a dying world. He went on a trip to Brighton to rest, and one day wrote in his journal, *"There the Lord conquered my unbelief, and I surrendered myself to God for this service. I told him that all responsibility as to the issues and consequences must rest with Him; that as his servant it was mine to obey and follow him. "*

China Inland Mission (CIM) was born. They were a new breed of missionaries. These missionaries would have no guaranteed salaries, nor could they appeal for funds; they would simply trust God to supply their needs; and its missionaries would wear Chinese clothing and then take the gospel into the interior of China.

The next year, Taylor, his wife, his four children, and sixteen young missionaries sailed from London to join five others already there. Years prior when he prepared to go to China the first time, he studied medicine. Now he was seeing two hundred patients a day. Some of the CIM missionaries left to join other missions, but in 1876, with fifty-two missionaries, CIM had one-fifth of the missionaries in China.

In 1881, he prayed for seventy missionaries, including unmarried women, and he got seventy-six. In 1886, he asked for one hundred and got 102. He had a radical style. Hudson wrote, *"China is not to be won for Christ by quiet, ease-loving men and women...The stamp of men and women we need is such as will put Jesus, China [and] souls first and foremost in everything and at every time - even life itself must be secondary."*

Though living in China took a large toll on the Taylor family—Hudson's wife died of cholera at age thirty-three; four of their eight children died before they reached the age of ten; and by 1900, his health was failing—CIM grew and prospered. He inspired thousands to leave behind the comforts of home and bring the message of Good News to the interior of China. With the communist takeover in 1949, the work was interrupted; however, CIM still continues today under the name Overseas Missionary Fellowship.

After Maria died, Hudson eventually remarried and had two more children. Jennie helped Hudson with his health issues and ministry. She ministered to women and helped him with the organization. She died in 1904, with Hudson following a year later.

What an inspiration Hudson Taylor is. His boldness never waned. He made a plan and set out to do it. Because of his tenacity, there are many thousands of people who have been told about the saving grace of God. Oh that I could have a fraction of his boldness.

WORDS OF
Hudson Taylor

"I am so weak that I cannot read my Bible
...even pray, I can only lie still in God's arms
like a little child and trust."

"Whatever is your best time of day,
give that to communion with God."

"I have found that there are 3 stages
in every great work of God:

1. it is impossible

2. it is difficult

3. it is done."

"The Great Commission
is not an option to be considered,
it is a command
to be obeyed."

*"All God's giants have been weak men
who did great things for God
because they reckoned on God being with them."*

———

*"Our joy in Him may be a fluctuating thing:
His joy in us knows no change."*

———

Fanny was the only child of John Crosby and his second wife Mercy Crosby, both of whom were relatives of Revolutionary War spy Enoch Crosby. He was a widower who had a daughter from his first marriage. It is possible that Fanny's parents were first cousins, which caused much embarrassment. She had a Puritan heritage and was a descendant of William Brewster, Edward Winslow, and Thomas Prence of the Mayflower.

She was also a member of the Daughters of the American Revolution. Bing and Bob Crosby were also relatives.

At six weeks old, Crosby caught a cold and developed inflammation of the eyes. Mustard poultices were applied to treat the discharges. According to Crosby, this procedure damaged her optic nerves and blinded her, but modern physicians think that her blindness was more likely congenital and, given her age, may simply not have been noticed by her parents.

Her father died in November 1820 when she was only six months old, so she was raised by her mother and maternal grandmother, Eunice Paddock Crosby. These women grounded her in Christian principles, helping her memorize long passages of the Bible.

When Crosby was three, the family moved to North Salem, New York, where Eunice had been raised. In April 1825, Fanny was examined by a surgeon who concluded that her condition was inoperable and that her blindness was permanent.

At the age of eight, Crosby wrote her first poem which described her condition. She later stated: "It seemed intended by the blessed providence of God that I should be blind all my life, and I thank Him for the dispensation. If perfect earthly sight were offered me tomorrow I would not accept it. I might not have sung hymns to the praise of God if I had been distracted by the beautiful and interesting things about me." She also once said, "when I get to Heaven, the first face that shall ever gladden my sight will be that of my Savior."

In 1828, Mercy and Fanny moved to the home of Mrs. Hawley in Ridgefield, Connecticut. While there, they attended the Presbyterian church on the village green. Crosby memorized five chapters of the Bible every week until she was ten, with the encouragement of her grandmother and later Mrs. Hawley; by age fifteen, she had memorized the four gospels, the Pentateuch, the Book of Proverbs, the Song of Solomon, and many of the Psalms. In 1832, a music teacher came to Ridgefield twice a week to give music lessons to her and some other children. Around the same time, she attended the Methodist Episcopal Church and loved the hymns.

In 1835, she enrolled in the New York Institution for the Blind (NYIB). She was fifteen years old. She was there for eight years as a student, then two more as a graduate student. During this time, she learned to play the piano, organ, harp, and guitar.

In 1843, Crosby joined some lobbyists in Washington, D.C., arguing for support of education of the blind. She was the first woman to speak in the United States Senate. She read a poem, and when she appeared before the joint houses of Congress, recited these lines:

> *O ye, who here from every state convene,*
>
> *Illustrious band! may we not hope the scene*
>
> *You now behold will prove to every mind*
>
> *Instruction hath a ray to cheer the blind.*

In 1844, she recited an original composition calling for an institution for educating the blind in every state, which was praised by John Quincy Adams. She continued speaking before notable people for several years and performed music at the White House for President Polk and his wife.

She joined the faculty at NYIB teaching grammar, rhetoric, and history. While teaching at the institute, she befriended seventeen-year-old Grover Cleveland, who later became President of the United States. She was a longtime member of Sixth Avenue Baptist Church in Brooklyn, New York. She wrote hymns and was very busy. There was a cholera epidemic in 1849, and she remained at the NYIB to help nurse the sick. She became worn and depressed. According to Bernard Ruffin: "In this atmosphere of death and gloom, Fanny became increasingly introspective over her soul's welfare. She began to realize that something was lacking in her spiritual life. She knew that she had gotten wrapped up in social, political, and educational reform, and did not have a sufficient love for God in her heart."

Crosby's earliest published poem was sent without her knowledge to P.T. Barnum, who published it in his *The Herald of Freedom*. Her inclination to write was encouraged by this experience. She began having more poems published and was inspired between 1851 and 1857 to write music. She co-wrote many minstrels, laments, and ballads. She also wrote many songs during the Civil War. In 1877, Crosby met William J. Kirkpatrick, one of the most prolific composers of gospel song tunes and "the most prominent publisher in the Wesleyan/Holiness Movement."

In the summer of 1843, Crosby met Alexander van Alstyne Jr., called Van by his friends. He also was blind and enrolled at the NYIB, where he was a casual acquaintance of Crosby and sometimes a student of hers. He became a teacher there also and during this time, the couple were engaged to be married in 1858. After their wedding, they moved to Maspeth, Queens, New York.

In 1859, they had a daughter named Frances who died in her sleep soon after birth. Crosby wrote the hymn, "Safe in the Arms of Jesus." After this, the couple moved around a lot. They never owned their own home, and whenever they got extra money, they would give away what was not necessary. They organized concerts and gave half the proceeds to aid the poor.

By 1880, they rarely lived together. Van traveled with her, and she said they had an amiable relationship. When he died, she said they loved each other until the end.

Crosby was "the most prolific of all nineteenth century American songwriters." It is estimated that books containing her lyrics sold one hundred million copies. She was given a flat fee of $1 or $2 per hymn because of the copyright laws of the time. Whenever she wrote a hymn, she prayed it would bring people to Christ. Crosby's hymns were popular because they made people reflect on their experiences and emotions concerning their relationship with Christ.

She was intentional in all she did: the number of hymns she wrote, the amount of scripture she memorized, the number of poor she gave to, and her work in missions. At age sixty, she made a new commitment to Christ to serve the poor and to devote the rest of her life to mission work. She wanted to be known for her mission work. Over a hundred years later, we think of her music. However, her music is also part of her mission work.

She died in Bridgeport of arteriosclerosis and a cerebral hemorrhage in 1915 at the age of ninety-four. Her family erected a very small tombstone at her request which read: "Aunt Fanny: She hath done what she could; Fanny Crosby."

On Sunday, March 26, 1905, Fanny Crosby Day was celebrated in churches of many denominations around the world. Crosby left money in her will for "the sheltering of the senior males who had no place to live, with these men to pay a nominal fee to the home for their living expenses." In 1923, the King's Daughters of the First Methodist Church of Bridgeport, Connecticut, honored Crosby's request to memorialize her by beginning to raise the additional funds needed to establish the Fanny Crosby Memorial Home for the Aged. It operated until 1996 when it became the Bridgeport Rescue Mission.

There are lists of other honors for this woman who led a humble but in-the-spotlight life. Her legacy continues today. She took steps to provide for people after she died. She did not just plan for the near future. She had a plan to extend her ministry to others.

What is amazing to me is that she did not let being blind stop her at all. She accomplished so much *because* she was blind. By memorizing scripture, learning instruments, and learning poetry, she intentionally prepared for what God would have for her to do. And many have been blessed by her music and mission work. What a great example of overcoming!

WORDS OF
Fanny Crosby

"Oh what a happy soul I am.
Although I cannot see, I
am resolved that in this world I shall be.
How many blessings I enjoy
that other people don't.
To weep or sigh, because I'm blind?
I cannot and I won't."

"It is not enough to have a song on your lips.
You must also have a song
in your heart."

***

"Chords that were broken
will vibrate once more."

***

"God will answer your prayers better than you think.
Of course, one will not always get exactly what he has
asked for, we all have sorrows and disappointments,
but one must never forget that if commended to God,
they will issue in good, His own solution
is far better than any we could conceive."

***

Redeemed, how I love to proclaim it!

Redeemed by the blood of the Lamb;

Redeemed through His infinite mercy,

His child, and faorever, I am.

***

HOWEVER WEAK WE ARE, HOWEVER
LITTLE OUR FAITH, OR HOWEVER SMALL
OUR GRACE MAY BE, OUR NAMES ARE
STILL WRITTEN ON HIS HEART; NOR SHALL
WE LOSE OUR SHARE IN JESUS' LOVE.
- CHARLES HADDON SPURGEON

CHAPTER 16

Charles Haddon Spurgeon
Preaching the Word

Charles Spurgeon was an English Particular Baptist preacher. Spurgeon remains highly influential among Christians of various denominations, among whom he is known as the "Prince of Preachers." He used simple language of ordinary speech. He was in opposition to the liberal and pragmatic theological tendencies in the Church of his day.

He was born June 19, 1834 in Kelvedon, Essex, England, and died January 31, 1892. Spurgeon authored sermons, an autobiography, commentaries, books on prayer, devotionals, magazines, poetry, and hymns. He was a powerful speaker and many of his sermons were translated into other languages.

Although he was born in Kelvedon, his family moved to Colchester when he was ten months old. In 1850, at age fifteen, he was on his way to an appointment and a snow storm forced him to shorten his journey.

He turned into a chapel in Newtown. God opened his heart to the gospel message. The text that influenced his decision was Isaiah 45:22,

> *"Look unto me,*
> *and be ye saved,*
> *all the ends of the earth,*
> *for I am God,*
> *and there is none else. "*

Later that year, he moved to Cambridge and became a Sunday school teacher. He preached his first sermon in a cottage in Teversham while filling in for a friend. And later that year, he was installed as pastor of the small Baptist church at Waterbeach, Cambridgeshire.

In 1854, at only nineteen years old, he became pastor of New Park Street Chapel, Southwark. This was the largest Baptist church in London at the time. And along with another fellow pastor, he founded the London Baptist Association.

Very soon, his ability as a preacher made him famous. By the time of his death in 1892, he had preached nearly 3,600 sermons and published forty-nine volumes of commentaries, sayings, and devotions.

He was also greatly criticized, mainly by the media. He was plain-spoken and had a direct appeal to the people, using the Bible to encourage people to always consider Jesus Christ. But his church continued to grow and they moved to a larger facility where he sometimes preached to ten thousand people. At the age of twenty-two, Spurgeon was the most popular preacher of the day.

On January 8, 1856, he married Susannah Thompson. At the end of that year during a sermon at his church, someone yelled, "Fire!" A stampede killed many. Spurgeon was emotionally devastated, and it had a sobering influence on the remainder of his life.

His work continued, and a Pastor's College was founded in 1857. It was renamed Spurgeon's College in 1923. In 1861, his congregation moved to the Metropolitan Tabernacle, which was the largest edifice of its day. He preached there several times a week until his death thirty-one years later. He never gave altar calls at the conclusion of his sermons, but told people they could always meet with him on Monday mornings. There was always someone at his door the next day.

He wrote his sermons out fully before he preached, but only used notes when he preached. Stenographers would take notes during each sermon and give them to him for revisions for publication. They remain one of the best series of writings in history. Hymns were also very important to him. They always sang without instruments during his services.

He became friends with Hudson Taylor and supported China Inland Mission and directed many missionary candidates to apply to the mission field in China. He also promoted the use of *The Wordless Book.*

Spurgeon founded the Stockwell Orphanage, which opened for boys in 1867 and for girls in 1879. It was bombed during WWII. The orphanage later became Spurgeon's Child Care Center and still exists today.

Spurgeon greatly disliked the watering down of scripture and new trains of thought that were taking away from the Bible. He opposed owning slaves. He stood up for his beliefs, and received life-threatening letters and lost support from Southern Baptists and many others.

Spurgeon suffered poor health at the end of his life, afflicted from a combination of rheumatism, gout, and Bright's disease. He died in Menton, France, where he often went to rest when he felt ill.

He was not thought of as a theologian, but his sermons were doctrinally sound. His sermons were very cross-centered. One of his favorite verses was John 12:32,

"And I, when I am lifted up from the earth,
will draw all people to myself."

He insisted on celebrating the Lord's Supper every Sunday and often during the week. Regeneration was one of his three Rs: ruin, redemption, and regeneration. A friend of his once came to him depressed because for three months of ministry, he had not seen a single conversion. Spurgeon slyly asked, "Do you expect the Lord to save souls every time you open your mouth?" Embarrassed, the man answered, "No, no sir!" "Then," Spurgeon replied, "that is just the reason why you have not had conversions: According to your faith be it unto you."

He saw regeneration as a work of pure grace. He felt that those the Lord regenerates, he will indwell. And "with such an indweller we need not fear, but that this poor heart of ours will yet become perfect as God is perfect; and our nature through His indwelling shall rise into complete meetness for the inheritance of the saints in light."

Spurgeon loved nature and God's creation and felt it refreshed the body.

He said, "A day's breathing of fresh air upon the hills, or a few hour's ramble in the beech woods' umbrageous calm, would sweep the cobwebs out of the brain of scores of our toiling ministers who are now but half alive. A mouthful of sea air, or a stiff walk in the wind's face, would not give grace to the soul, but it would yield oxygen to the body, which is next best."

People felt he had a bubbly personality and he often caused them to laugh. An entire chapter in his autobiography is entitled "Pure Fun." To him, joy was a manifestation of the happiness and cheer found in Christ alone, even though he also suffered from sadness from personal tragedy like all people.

Charles Spurgeon died at fifty-seven, yet remains one of the most notable men in the past two hundred years. He enjoyed life and loved telling others about Christ. He was purposeful and bold. He stood for what was right and never wavered, even when opposed. He is also one of the most quoted people of all time. Why? I think because what he said still rings true. It resonates with what we believe without being full of nonsense. He was criticized for being too plain and straightforward, yet his books are still sought after 150 years later.

WORDS OF
Charles Haddon Spurgeon

"How sweet is it to learn the Savior's love
when nobody else loves us!
When friends flee, what a blessed thing it is to see
that the Savior does not forsake us
but still keeps us and holds us fast
and clings to us and will not let us go!"

"You are no saint, says the devil.
Well, if I am not, I am a sinner,
and Jesus Christ came into the world
to save sinners.
Sink or swim, I go to Him;
other hope, I have none."

———

"If Christ has died for me,
ungodly as I am,
then I cannot live in sin
any longer but must arouse myself
to love and serve Him
who has redeemed me."

———

"The greatest enemy to the human soul
is the self-righteous spirit
which makes men look
to themselves for salvation."

———

"By perseverance the snail reached the ark."

———

"Many men owe the grandeur of their lives
to their tremendous difficulties."

———

GIVE ME THE LOVE THAT
LEADS THE WAY...
- AMY CARMICHAEL

CHAPTER 17

Amy Carmichael

"Amma"

Amy Beatrice Carmichael was an Irish Christian missionary in India who opened an orphanage and founded a mission in Dohnavur. She served in India fifty-five years without furlough (or leaving India) and wrote many books about missionary work there. She was born December 16, 1867 in Millisle, United Kingdom, and died January 18, 1951 in Dohnavur. She was the oldest of seven siblings. Her parents were both devout Christians. She attended Harrogate Ladies College for four years in her youth.

When she was sixteen, her family moved to Belfast. Her father died two years later. They founded the Welcome Evangelical Church, and in the 1880s, she began a class for young women. This class grew to two hundred, and she saw an opportunity to purchase property and build a larger facility. After the death of her father, her family faced bankruptcy after a couple years, so they decided to move to Manchester. She started working in the slum areas. She attended a convention and heard Hudson Taylor speak about the China Inland Mission. She became convinced of her calling to missionary work to share the gospel overseas and help those in need.

Amy worked with the Church Missionary Society and eventually arrived in Bangalore in India. It was here she discovered her lifelong passion—reaching out to girls and young women sold as slaves to the Hindu temple priests.

She founded the Dohnavur Fellowship in 1901 in Tamil Nadu, thirty miles from India's southern tip. It became a sanctuary for over one thousand children who called her "Amma," which means "mother."

To help herself fit in, she dressed in Indian clothes, dyed her skin with coffee, and often traveled long distances to save just one child from suffering. In 1912, Queen Mary recognized the mission's work and helped fund a hospital at Dohnavur. By the following year, the Dohnavur Fellowship served 130 girls and later opened the doors to young boys.

Amy's legacy continues in the Dohnavur Fellowship, which remains in existence today.

She has written many books including *God's Missionary* and *Edges of His Ways.* Before she died, she requested no stone be put over her grave, but the children put a birdbath with the inscription, "Amma."

When I was in college, someone gave me the book *If* by Amy Carmichael. At the time, I had no clue why. I had some things I was dealing with, and now I can guess why. I kept that book for years. I just went to look for it, but couldn't find it. I must have given it to someone over the years.

This book, like her others, is to point people to the Cross and how much God loves us and how we then can love others. I certainly think she was a person of such conviction and purpose. She served all her adult life. She was an amazing selfless woman.

WORDS OF
Amy Carmichael

"If I say, 'Yes, I forgive,
but I cannot forget,'
as though the God,
who twice a day
washes all the sands
on all the shores of all the world,
could not wash such memories
from my mind,
then I know nothing of Calvary love."

"If I covet any place on earth but the
dust at the foot of the cross,
then I know nothing of Calvary's love."

"If I fear to hold another to the highest goal
because it is so much easier to avoid doing so,
then I know nothing of Calvary's love."

"How can we follow the Savior far,
who have no wound or scar?"

"There are many rooms in the house of pain."

*"You can give without loving,
but you cannot love without giving."*

*"We have all eternity to celebrate the victories
but only a few hours before sunset to win them."*

SO, IF WE ONLY LEAD ONE SOUL TO CHRIST, WE MAY SET A STREAM IN MOTION THAT WILL FLOW ON WHEN WE ARE DEAD AND GONE ...
- D.L. MOODY

CHAPTER 18

Dwight L. Moody

Evangelistic Endeavors

"THE BIBLE WILL KEEP YOU FROM SIN,
OR SIN WILL KEEP YOU FROM THE BIBLE."

I wrote this quote in my Bible as a teen and in every Bible since. I never knew who said it until now. It just stuck with me. Through the last forty years, I have met many people who got their college degree from Moody Bible Institute. I knew it stood firm on serving God and always knew it to be a great place. I had read a few things through the years about the man behind the school, and in planning out this section of this book, I thought he would be a great person to research.

I discovered he also founded Moody Church, Northfield School and Mount Hermon School in Massachusetts, and Moody Publishers. That is a lot to accomplish in one lifetime. Dwight L. Moody was born on February 5, 1837 and lived until December 22, 1899. In his early years, he had a boot and shoe business. He had been the seventh child in a large family.

One month after the final children, who were twins, were born, his father died. This happened when Moody was four. They were poor and several of the children went elsewhere to work for room and board. Their mother sent them to church. When he was seventeen, Dwight moved to Boston to work. He apprenticed for a man there. The man required him to go to church with him. Soon after, he became a Christian. This conversion gave him an interest in evangelism.

He wanted to give his life to revivalism. Revivalism was wanting to merge the theological and institutional practices of evangelical Protestantism with the new urban environment created by industrialism. He worked with the men in the Civil War through the YMCA. After the war, he had a church in Chicago, but it burnt down in The Great Chicago Fire in 1871. He ended up purchasing a home in Northfield, Massachusetts, near his birthplace. He decided to have summer conferences there and had speakers from all around the world.

Moody continued with his evangelistic work and wanted to help with cross-cultural evangelism by promoting *The Wordless Book,* a teaching tool developed in 1866 by Charles Spurgeon. In 1875, Moody added a fifth color to the design: gold, which represented Heaven.

- **GOLD REMINDS US OF HEAVEN.** *God wants us to be with Him in Heaven.*

- **THE DARK PAGE REMINDS US OF SIN.** *Because we have all sinned, we cannot get to heaven on our own.*

- **RED REMINDS US OF THE BLOOD OF JESUS.** *Jesus came to earth to take the punishment for our sins by dying on the cross.*

- *THE CLEAN PAGE REMINDS US THAT WE CAN BE MADE CLEAN FROM SIN BY BELIEVING IN JESUS. When we believe in Jesus, we can have a relationship with God and will one day be with Him in heaven.*

- *GREEN REMINDS US OF THINGS THAT GROW. It is important that we grow in our relationship with Jesus.*

This book continues today to teach children around the world about the gospel.

He was also the author of many books, including *Christ In You, Heaven, Men God Challenged, and Spiritual Power.* His life is also written about in *A Passion For Souls: The Life of D. L. Moody* by Lyle Dorsett.

Moody was influenced by Hudson Taylor. He supported China Inland Mission and encouraged his congregation to serve in overseas mission work.

He died in 1899. He was known as a "dynamo of energy." In his honor, ten years after his death, the Chicago Avenue Church was renamed the Moody Church. And the Chicago Bible Institute was named the Moody Bible Institute.

He was so well thought of and people always knew where he stood on things. He spent many years serving God and letting others know God loved them. He encouraged believers to serve. I can tell reading many quotes from him how he wanted believers to know God with all their heart. He also wanted them to serve, not just to have Bible knowledge in their head. There was no partiality with him, and he wanted believers to reach out cross-culturally. He was bold in sharing his faith and wanted others to also do so.

WORDS OF
Dwight L. Moody

*"God doesn't seek for golden vessels,
and does not ask for silver ones,
but He must have clean ones."*

*"When I read the life of such a man as Paul,
how I blush to think how sickly and dwarfed
Christianity is at the present time,
and how many hundreds there are who never think of
working for the Son of God and honoring Christ."*

*"The last business of Christ's life
was the saving of a poor penitent thief."*

*"If Jesus bore the cross, and died on it for me,
ought I not to be willing to take it up for Him?"*

*"I should like to see a wave surging
from Maine to California
sweeping thousands into the Kingdom of God."*

DO NOT BE AFRAID...
READ THE LAST PAGES OF THE BIBLE:
JESUS IS VICTOR!
- CORRIE TEN BOOM

CHAPTER 19

Corrie ten Boom

Taking Action

My sweet Moma read her Corrie ten Boom book almost every day in her later years. I would visit her and sit on her bed and she would take her Bible, her *Our Daily Bread,* and her Corrie ten Boom book *Each New Day* from her nightstand and sit herself on the edge of her bed and read aloud. My sister had the privilege of hearing this for years, since she took care of her. I knew who Corrie ten Boom was of course. I had read *The Hiding Place* forty years previously when I was in college. I thought it was amazing, but I do not think I REALLY grasped its full meaning or appreciated it. Moma would put a bookmark in the book each night. The last bookmark was in October—Moma died in November at age ninety-seven. No matter how difficult, she read every night up until a month before she died.

Here is a quote from one of the devotionals:

> *"If you truly love your fellow man, you must warn him of the danger of losing eternal life. Tell everyone*

you can reach the glorious story of Jesus, that they may be saved in time. The world is full of people who need salvation. It is our job to find them and deliver the message. 'There is salvation in no one else, for there is no other name under heaven given among men by which we must be saved.' Acts 4:12 RSV Holy Spirit, help us not to lose one opportunity."

Can you sense the urgency? The copyright on this was 1977, long after WWII. Let us backtrack our story to get the full picture.

Cornelia Arnolda Johanna "Corrie" was Dutch, born in 1892 in Haarlem, Netherlands. She had three older siblings: Betsie, Willem, and Nollie. Her father was a watchmaker. Their family lived above the watch shop. After her sister Betsie became sick for an extended time, Corrie began working with her father. She loved the business and by 1922, became the first woman to be licensed as a watchmaker in the Netherlands. Her family belonged to the Calvinist Christians within the Dutch Reformed Church. She later established a club for teenage girls, teaching them sewing and other handcrafts. Her faith was strong, and her parents and church instructed the children that all people were created equal. They had a soft spot for Jews.

In May 1940, the German army had invaded the Netherlands. Corrie's youth organization for women was banned. A person came to their home because they heard the ten Booms loved Jews. The woman was fearful because she was a Jew. Corrie's father believed the Jews were God's chosen people, so they welcomed the woman. The family then became active in the Dutch Underground. They opened their home to the refugees and were members of the resistance movement. Because of this, an architect came to their home to build a secret room with a bell letting the people know when the Gestapo was nearby. Food was scarce. Everyone received a ration card. Corrie became the leader of a network that smuggled Jews to safe places. It is estimated that they were able to save approximately eight hundred Jews.

In February 1944, a Dutch informant, Jan Vogel, told the Nazis about the ten Booms' work. They arrested the entire ten Boom family. They were sent to Scheveningen Prison. Nollie and Willem were immediately released. Their father died within ten days. Six people who were in the secret room were not found. Corrie was initially put into solitary confinement. At her hearing, she shared about helping mentally disabled people; the Nazis had been killing the mentally disabled for years.

Corrie and Betsie eventually were sent to Ravensbruck concentration camp, a women's labor camp in Germany. They held worship services using a Bible someone had managed to smuggle in. Many accepted Christ as their savior. By December, Betsie's health began failing and she died on December 16. Before she died, she told Corrie, "There is no pit so deep that He (God) is not deeper still." Twelve days later, Corrie was released. She was later told that it was an error. Corrie later found out that the rest of the women in her age group were sent to the gas chambers a week later.

Corrie helped many in need of healing and help after the war. She knew people needed help in overcoming the psychological scars left by Nazi occupation. She returned to Germany in 1946 and forgave two Germans who had worked at Ravensbruck. One had been particularly cruel to Betsie. Corrie began her public speaking in more than sixty countries. She wrote several books. The Hiding Place was made into a movie. In 1978, she suffered two strokes. Then later in 1983, after a third stroke, she died.

Being bold does not describe the bravery it took for this family to help others in need. They took action and did what they knew God would have them do: Help others. They knew what the Nazis were doing was evil. They took big steps by building a safe place for those in danger. Betsie and Corrie encouraged the other women in prison. They did not know if they would ever survive. And then, after the war, Corrie intentionally went on to share the hope God gives, no matter what circumstances we find ourselves in. She devoted her entire life to others. She is a great example to us all.

WORDS OF
Corrie ten Boom

"Any concern too small to be turned into prayer is too small to be made into a burden."

"Let God's promises shine on your problems."

"When a train goes through a tunnel and it gets dark, you don't throw away the ticket and jump off. You sit still and trust the engineer."

"Never be afraid to trust an unknown future to a known God."

"Memories are the key not to the past, but to the future. I know that the experiences of our lives, when we let God use them, become the mysterious and perfect preparation for the work He will give us to do."

*GOD HAS GIVEN US TWO HANDS –
ONE TO RECEIVE WITH AND THE
OTHER TO GIVE WITH. WE ARE NOT
CISTERNS MADE FOR HOARDING; WE
ARE CHANNELS MADE FOR SHARING.
– BILLY GRAHAM*

CHAPTER 20

The Reverend Billy Graham

Sharing Christ

When one thinks of the greatest evangelists of all time, they often think about Wesley, Whitfield, Edwards, Calvin, or even Billy Sunday. These were all great men and had a deep concern for the lost, but in more modern times, I often think about Billy Graham. He was called "America's pastor," but he was truly a great evangelist. One biographer called him the most influential Christian leader of the twentieth century.

According to his website, he preached to live audiences of 210 million people in more than 185 countries. He was a spiritual advisor to presidents and other pastors and evangelists. Gallup's list of most admired men and women had him listed sixty-one times, which was a record.

Billy was born November 7, 1918 in Charlotte, North Carolina. He was raised on a dairy farm with his two sisters, brother, and parents. In his childhood, he loved reading, and his favorite stories were about

Tarzan. Some said this helped him become a minister so he could have a loud voice.

In 1934, he was converted at a series of revival meetings. He graduated from high school in 1936, and went on to attend Bob Jones University. He felt the rules and regulations were too restrictive and was almost expelled for breaking so many rules. However, a leader there told him he had "a voice that pulls" and God could use it mightily. He then transferred to Temple Bible Institute in Florida. He would paddle a canoe to a small island and practice preaching to the birds and animals. Graham was ordained by a group of Southern Baptist clergy in Florida. He then went to Wheaton College in Illinois where he graduated. During his time there, he pastored a church and launched a radio ministry called *Songs In The Night*. Graham recruited George Beverly Shea as the director of his show. The ministry continued for many years, but by 1945, Graham decided to move on.

His first evangelistic crusade was in September 1947 in Grand Rapids, Michigan. It was attended by six thousand people. He was twenty-eight years old. He would invite people to come forward where they could speak to a counselor. They could speak one-on-one and have any questions answered. They were given a gospel of John and a Bible study booklet.

In 1948, he became president of Northwestern Bible College in Minneapolis. He resigned in 1952. Graham traveled as a youth evangelist for Youth For Christ. He did this for many years in both the United States and Europe. His giftedness as an evangelist became evident.

During 1949, he scheduled a series of revival meetings in Los Angeles. He put circus tents in a parking lot. This attracted national media coverage. Although he originally scheduled this for three weeks, it ended up going for eight weeks. He became a national figure. The pianist, Rudy Atwood, who played at the meetings, wrote that this "rocketed Billy Graham into national prominence, and resulted in the conversion of a number of show-business personalities."

In Durbin, South Africa, in 1973, the crowd was approximately one hundred thousand. This was the largest group gathering since apartheid. He never wavered in his boldness and told the crowd that apartheid was sin. In Moscow in 1992, a quarter of the one hundred and fifty-five thousand people went forward to accept Christ. His favorite song during his crusades was "Just As I Am." He continued his crusades in London for twelve weeks and Madison Square Garden for sixteen weeks.

He loved speaking to college students and traveled to many campuses asking them to turn their lives over to Christ. Many times as he traveled in the South during segregation, there would be ropes separating people. Graham began by tearing down the ropes. He was quoted in one revival as saying, "We have been proud and thought we were better than any other race, any other people. Ladies and gentlemen, we are going to stumble into hell because of our pride."

He also told a member of the Ku Klux Klan, "There is no scriptural basis for segregation. The ground at the foot of the cross is level, and it touches my heart when I see whites standing shoulder to shoulder with blacks at the cross."

In 1974, Graham invited John Stott to write *The Lausanne Covenant*, which helped challenge and unite evangelical Christians in the task of world evangelism. This was a significant fruit of Graham's legacy.

Graham continued his evangelistic career for many years, but by 1992, his health began failing. He suffered from hydrocephalus. In April 2010, then ninety-one, he had hearing and vision loss and difficulty with his balance. He died on February 21, 2018 at the age of ninety-nine.

Billy Graham lived life to the fullest. No wasted time, but "redeeming the time." He was quoted as saying, "Being a Christian is more than just an instantaneous conversion - it is a daily process whereby you grow to be more and more like Christ."

He had a burden for the lost and felt that burning desire within to share the plan of salvation with everyone. I admit that while I have prayed for loved ones to accept Christ and that I would share with those I come in contact with, I fall short of the determined planned path to go out with great purpose and share with this kind of boldness. I encourage you, dear reader, to pray for opportunities to share your faith.

WORDS OF
Billy Graham

*"My home is in Heaven.
I'm just traveling through this world."*

*"I've read the last page of the Bible.
It's all going to turn out all right."*

*"Courage is contagious.
When a brave man takes a stand,
the spines of others are often stiffened."*

"I just want to lobby for God."

⁓

"A real Christian is a person who
can give his pet parrot to the town gossip."

⁓

"You cannot pray for someone
and hate them at the same time."

⁓

"Do you want your faith to grow?
Then let the Bible begin to
saturate your mind and soul."

⁓

"You cannot build a superstructure
on a cracked foundation."

⁓

SOMETIMES...
FEAR DOES NOT SUBSIDE AND...
ONE MUST CHOOSE TO DO IT AFRAID.
- ELISABETH ELLIOT

CHAPTER 21

Jim and Elisabeth Elliot

Giving Their All

W hen I think of a group of people who gave their all for Christ, the group of five couples who went to Ecuador to minister to the unreached Auca tribe top my list. The Aucas had killed all outsiders who had been to that area. They knew it was a dangerous thing to do, but felt that God had led them to that place. They, like many other heroes of faith, felt an urgent need to share the gospel.

Jim Elliot, who grew up in Oregon, loved when missionaries shared at his church while he was growing up. He asked questions of them and determined in his heart that he too one day would go to a faraway place and share the gospel. In February 1952, Jim Elliot, along with fellow missionary Pete Fleming, left for Ecuador to study language in Quito. They learned Spanish well. Then they decided to move to the jungle. They spent three years sharing their faith with the Quechua Indian village. Many accepted Christ and were growing in their faith. Now Jim felt it was the time to move to help the Aucas. Their tribe had killed many of the Quechua tribe and men who worked for the local oil company. Jim and four other missionaries made a plan to go to the Aucas and show them that they were friendly.

Nate Saint, who was a missionary supply pilot, began lowering a supply bucket to the tribe. He felt this would be a safe way to contact them. After several months, the Aucas sent a gift back up in the basket. The missionaries decided it was finally time to meet the Aucas in person. They spotted a beach they felt would be a good place to meet. They built a treehouse near the Curaray River to keep themselves safe. Then one day, Nate flew over the village and encouraged the Aucas to come to the beach. Two women and a man showed up. Nate took the man up in the plane and they all shared a meal together. The missionaries felt a friendship had begun.

They encouraged more Aucas to come. They waited for several days. Finally, on day six, two women came out of the jungle, then immediately retreated. A group of warriors with spears raised came running toward the missionaries. All five men, Ed McCully, Roger Youderian, Nate Saint, Pete Fleming, and Jim Elliot died that day.

That afternoon of Sunday, January 8, 1956, Elisabeth Elliot, Jim's wife, waited by her two-way radio. The wives grew worried. Another missionary pilot flew over the beach and only saw the plane. The United States sent a search team and found the bodies.

Operation Auca was not a failure. Many Aucas became Christians through what they had learned from other missionaries and the continued care of those who had lost so much, but still wanted to share the gospel with them. Elisabeth and Nate's sister, Rachel, continued to minister to the Aucas. Two years after the death of their loved ones, these women moved into the village. They were now a friendly tribe.

Elisabeth went on to do evangelistic work and wrote the books, *Shadow of the Almighty: The Life and Testament of Jim Elliot* and *Through Gates of Splendor.* She even helped in the making of the movie *Through Gates of Splendor,* based on her book that she had written about their tragedy. Jim Elliot had wanted many others to become missionaries. Through his death, many did.

In Jim's journal entry for October 28, 1949, he states that his work for Jesus counted more than his life. He wrote, *"He is no fool who gives what he cannot keep to gain that which he cannot lose."* His quote is from Luke 9:24, which reads,

"For whosoever will save his life shall lose it:
whosoever will lose his life for my sake, the same shall save it."

Then he wrote a citation from Luke 16:9,

"...that when it shall fail,
they may receive you into everlasting habitations."

Elisabeth spent two years ministering to the tribe that killed her husband. She is one of the most influential women of the twentieth century. She remained faithful despite extremely difficult trials. While she lived in Ecuador after Jim's death, she learned why the tribesmen killed her husband. This is a quote from her about that time, *"The Auca was trying to preserve his own way of life, his own liberty. He believed the foreigners were a threat to that liberty, so he feels he had every right to kill them. In America, we decorate a man for defending his country."*

She went on to be a speaker and author and started a foundation. She also taught at Gordon-Conwell Theological Seminary. Elisabeth wanted believers to see others as God sees them. In her book, *Passion and Purity,* she says, *"Our vision is so limited, we can hardly imagine a love that does not show itself in protection from suffering. The love of God is of a different nature altogether. It does not hate tragedy. It never denies reality. It stands in the very teeth of suffering. The love of God did not protect his own Son. That was the proof of love—That He gave that Son, that he let him go to Calvary's cross, though 'legions of angels' might have rescued Him."*

She lived her life to the fullest and inspired many.

WORDS OF
Elisabeth Elliot

"We can hardly imagine a love that does not show itself in protection from suffering.
The love of God is of a different nature altogether.
It does not hate tragedy.
It never denies reality.
It stands in the very teeth of suffering."

"The fact is, as believers, it is not about us.
It is not about my happiness, my joy, my wellbeing.
It is about the glory of God and the kingdom of Christ.
The only means to real joy and contentment
is to make His glory the supreme objective in my life."

"The fact that I am a woman does not
make me a different kind of Christian,
but the fact that I am a Christian
makes me a different kind of woman.

Do The Next Thing

From an old English parsonage, down by the sea

There came in the twilight a message to me;

Its quaint Saxon legend, deeply engraven,

Hath, as it seems to me, teaching from Heaven.

And on through the hours the quiet words ring

Like a low inspiration Do the next thing!

Many a questioning, many a fear,

Many a doubt, hath its quieting here.

Moment by moment, let down from Heaven,

Time, opportunity, guidance, are given.

Fear not tomorrow, Child of the King,

Trust them with Jesus,

Do the next thing!

Do it immediately; do it with prayer;

Do it reliantly, casting all care;

Do it with reverence, tracing His Hand

Who placed it before thee with earnest command.

Stayed on Omnipotence,

safe 'neath His wing,

Leave all resultings,

Do the next thing!

Looking to Jesus, ever serener,

Working or suffering—be thy demeanor,

In His dear Presence, the rest of His calm,

The light of His countenance be thy psalm,

Strong in His faithfulness, praise and sing,

Then as He beckons thee

Do the next thing!

Bold: 1.   showing an ability to take risks; confident and courageous,

2.   having a strong appearance

"Since we have such a hope,
we are very bold."

2 CORINTHIANS 3:12 (ESV)

BOLD &
THE BIBLE

PHOTO BY JAMIE HUDSON

...AS FOR ME AND MY HOUSE,
WE WILL SERVE THE LORD.
JOSHUA 24:15

CHAPTER 22

Joshua, Rahab, and the Spies

Confidence in the Lord

I love the book of Joshua. You feel that sense of excitement when the Israelites cross over into the land, land flowing with milk and honey. And then there is Rahab and the spies. It is an adventurous book. Cities of refuge and the Promised Land are definitely exciting events. Joshua had been Moses' understudy since he was a youth. The name "Joshua" means "Jehovah saves" or "The LORD is salvation." Joshua was commissioned by Moses and was filled with the spirit of wisdom as stated in Deuteronomy 34:9,

> *"Now Joshua the son of Nun was filled with the spirit of wisdom, for Moses had laid his hands on him; and the sons of Israel listened to him and did as the LORD had commanded Moses."*

Joshua was born in Egyptian slavery and was trained by Moses. The book of Joshua is the fulfillment of the promise of giving the land to Abraham's descendants. Joshua was a selfless man, wholly following what the Lord wanted him to do. We see a command from God to him in the very first chapter of Joshua, verses 1-6 and 9.

> *"Now it came about after the death of Moses the servant of the LORD that the LORD spoke to Joshua the son of Nun, Moses' servant, saying, 'Moses My servant is dead; now therefore arise, cross the Jordan, you and all this people, to the land which I am giving them, to the sons of Israel. Every place on which the sole of your foot treads, I have given it to you, just as I spoke to Moses. From the wilderness and this Lebanon, even as far as the great river, the river Euphrates, all the land of the Hittites, and as far as the Great Sea toward the setting of the sun, will be your territory. No man will be able to stand before you all the days of your life. Just as I have been with Moses, I will be with you; I will not fail you or forsake you." vs. 9, "Be strong and courageous! Do not tremble or be dismayed, for the LORD your God is with you wherever you go."*

In order for Joshua to cross the Jordan River, a lot had to take place. He began by sending out scouts to spy in the land and the city of Jericho. It would be their duty to collect information to assist the tribes of Israel to invade and conquer the land that was given to them by God. These men needed to let Joshua know about food, topography, and other things needed to be able to overcome the current inhabitants. So the spies looked for a place where they would be inconspicuous. And they also needed to have a quick getaway if needed. They decided to look for something on the city wall.

They came to the house of Rahab, a harlot whose home was near the gate. This house would be a good cover. Rahab had spent her entire adult life selling herself for evil purposes. She was as immoral as one can be, but this story is not about how hopeless she is, but about God's redemption and her new faith. It is true that she may never have met an Israelite before that day, but she had heard plenty. She knew of God helping the Israelites safely cross the Red Sea and what happened to Pharaoh's army. She knew Israel had wandered in the wilderness, and most likely had heard that they were now camped across the river. She knew that God would help them get across. So not only did she help the two men who came to her home on the city wall, but she would risk her life to do so.

Rahab was the product of a corrupt culture. The Israelite spies were not there to take advantage of her, but used her house on the wall to take measurements and find a strategy to help in the coming battle. Maybe this is why they gained her trust. And the spies were there for a reason. God wanted them there to show His grace. Rahab would be a great example of His saving faith, since she was at the bottom of the social ladder. And by God's providence, she ends up in the Messianic line in the genealogy of Jesus. She is named in the great faith chapter in Hebrews 11:31,

> *"By faith Rahab the harlot did not perish along with those who were disobedient, after she had welcomed the spies in peace."*

Rahab hid the men so the soldiers could not find them. Then Rahab tells a lie in Joshua 2:3-5,

"And the king of Jericho sent word to Rahab saying, 'Bring out the men who have come to you, who have entered your house, for they have come to search out the land.' But the woman had taken the two men and hidden them, and she said, 'Yes, the men came to me, but I did not know where they were from. And it came about when it was time to shut the gate, at dark, that the men went out; I do not know where the men went. Pursue them quickly, for you will overtake them.'

Then she goes up to the roof and tells the spies that she knows the LORD had given them the land. She had heard of Moses crossing the Red Sea on dry land. And in verses 11-13, she says,

"And when we heard it, our hearts melted and no courage remained in any man any longer because of you; for the LORD your God, He is God in heaven above and on earth beneath. Now therefore, please swear to me by the LORD, since I have dealt kindly with you, that you will deal kindly with my father's household, and give me a pledge of truth, and spare my father and my mother and my brothers and my sisters, with all who belong to them, and deliver our lives from death.'"

Not only does Rahab save the lives of the two spies, but also the lives of her family and their households. She bravely pleads their case before these men. I think she also thought quickly when the soldiers came and questioned her, although God does not condone lying. None of us are without sin, yet God still uses us. God honors her bravery, and her household is not harmed. He commends her faith, not her lying. The spies tell her to hang a red rope out her window so that when the men came to destroy the city, her household would be saved.

When the men returned to Joshua after spying out the land, verse 24 tells us,

> *"And they said to Joshua, 'Surely the LORD has given all the land into our hands, and all the inhabitants of the land, moreover, have melted away before us.'"*

Sometimes when we read through the Bible, we focus on the main characters, but so often the ripple effect of the events goes far beyond them. We don't even know the names of the two men sent to spy out the land. But they see God's protection and sovereign plan unfolding. They know beyond a shadow of a doubt that God is alive and that He is sufficient for their future.

The story continues as Joshua prepares for the crossing of the Jordan. I love the LORD assuring Joshua, yet again, that he is with him. In 3:7-9, we read,

> *"Now the LORD said to Joshua, 'This day I will begin to exalt you in the sight of all Israel, that they may know that just as I have been with Moses, I will be with you. You shall, moreover, command the priests who are carrying the ark of the covenant, saying, 'When you come to the edge of the waters of the Jordan, you shall stand still in the Jordan,' Then Joshua said to*

the sons of Israel, 'Come here, and hear the words of the LORD your God.'"

They did as the LORD commanded and crossed the Jordan on dry land. The next step was to capture Jericho. The fall of Jericho is a favorite story among kids. But these great documented truths are so important to teach us—both children and adults—about how we can live boldly for God and trust Him in all steps of life.

God gave Joshua detailed instructions on how to overcome Jericho and He also provided military support to help. The men were to march once around the city along with the Ark of the Covenant for six days. Seven priests carried seven trumpets made from ram's horns. Then on the seventh day, they marched around the city seven times, and on the seventh time when the people heard the ram's horn, they gave a great shout and the walls fell down. The LORD gave them the city.

The walls fell around the entire city, except where Rahab's house was. She and her household were spared, just as she requested. All the others along the wall and in the entire city were destroyed. She lived out her life with the Israelites and did not return to her former way of life, but received new life in God.

In the book of James in the New Testament, James writes about faith and works, and in 2:24-26, he says,

> *"You see that a man is justified by works, and not by faith alone. And in the same way was not Rahab the harlot also justified by works, when she received the messengers and sent them out by another way? For*

just as the body without the spirit is dead, so also faith without works is dead."

Dear reader, we too can act on our faith. If we are confident in knowing who God is and obedient to what God has for us, we too can be conquerors, because He loves us. In Genesis 15, God told Abraham that after four hundred years of being enslaved in another country, his descendants would return to the land God had promised them. After forty years of wandering in the wilderness, only Joshua and Caleb survived as leaders. All the other leaders died before entering the Promised Land, even Moses. God had big plans for Joshua and Caleb.

When we are obedient in our faith, God shows us what we can do to share that faith with others. We can show His love and power to others as we show our confidence in the LORD.

Rahab was not redeemed because of anything she did, but because of her faith. She knew the God who parted the sea could keep her safe from harm. She acted on that faith. She was confident in God and took bold action. She is a lesson on how faith in God can change us, no matter our past circumstances.

THEN HANNAH PRAYED AND SAID,
'MY HEART REJOICES IN THE LORD:
MY HORN IS EXALTED IN THE LORD.
I SMILE AT MY ENEMIES. BECAUSE I
REJOICE IN YOUR SALVATION.'
I SAMUEL 2:1 NKJV

CHAPTER 23

Hannah

Praying with Purpose

H annah was the essence of a woman of grace and dignity. She was supportive of her husband despite difficult situations, and became the very embodiment of true motherhood. Let us study a bit about this woman who prayed with purpose for years, not wavering in her belief and love for her LORD.

Hannah was childless and despaired of ever being a mother. She had the added stress that her husband, Elkanah, married a second wife so he could have children. In those days, in order to keep the family's land, you had to have children to pass it down to. So not only did she suffer from much sadness, but her husband's second wife taunted her about the fact that she had no children.

Hannah loved her husband and he loved her. Of course, this made for an even bigger rivalry between the women. Peninnah, Elkanah's other wife, had children and this caused Hannah constant anguish.

You can see Hannah's heart for God in her song. How thankful she is. She has a deep love for her Lord. They are amazing words of praise.

Hannah is very committed to her home and family. She has a deep love for her husband, and she wants to spend as much time as possible with her son. Remember, she committed him to service. This means Samuel would only be at home until he was about four. Once he goes away to the tabernacle to study and live, she visits him at least once a year when she makes him a robe and takes it to him.

Hannah is blessed with five more children: three sons and two daughters. Her persistence in prayer is a great example for us today. She prayed for a son, and God answered her prayers over and above her expectations.

Years ago, there was an article written entitled, "When Ma Wouldn't Give Up". I know this family and their heritage. I am close to the granddaughter. This was a large family of eleven children. The pa was an alcoholic: he had taken up social drinking because of his business, and neglected his family. Everyone would tell the ma that she should leave him. But she prayed faithfully every night for years. The youngest child, little Johnny, knew of a revival meeting across the train tracks nearby and wanted so badly for his dad to go.

He asked, "Will you take me too, Pa?"

He responded, "Sure Johnny, let's go."

He hesitated when they got near the community center and he heard them singing, "Whiter than snow." He turned to Johnny and said, "Johnny let's go home, and tomorrow night, I'll get all cleaned up and we'll come back."

"No, Pa, no! Let's go in now!" They finally went in and were seated.

The man preaching that night had been a drinking buddy of Pa's. Without hesitation, Pa's old buddy, Bob, walked from behind the pulpit and came down the aisle and exclaimed, "John!" and put his arm around Pa's shoulders. "John, you know as well as anybody the kind of life I used to live. But, look! What God has done for me, He can do for you. Come on, John, come with me."

John walked to the altar, knelt, and cried out to God, "God, be merciful to me, a sinner."

When they arrived home, he put his arms around Ma and said, "Sophie, you've got a new husband from tonight on."

Before he could tell her about what had happened in the gospel meeting, Ma cried out happily, "God has kept His promise! I knew He wouldn't fail!"

Through the years, most all the children, grandchildren, and great-grandchildren went into ministry. Ma never gave up. She was a woman of steel. She faithfully prayed for her husband. God rewarded her with a legacy she never dreamed of. She prayed with purpose for her family. She knew what to do and did it just like Hannah.

...HE RAISED UP DAVID TO BE THEIR KING,
CONCERNING WHOM HE ALSO TESTIFIED
AND SAID, 'I HAVE FOUND DAVID THE SON
OF JESSE, A MAN AFTER MY HEART, WHO
WILL DO ALL MY WILL.'
ACTS 13:22

CHAPTER 24

David

A Man After God's Own Heart

There are not many stories in the Bible as well known as David and Goliath. I think most people can remember seeing a drawing or painting of this story when they were a child. And the visual of the giant Philistine and the wee boy David typifies the title of this book. As we delve into some background on David, we will see this is not the last time he is bold and courageous, but only the beginning of his documented life as a fearless leader.

And so it begins. We have to first look at the prophet Samuel to fully understand the background of the story. Samuel had anointed Saul as king, but King Saul did not obey God. In 1 Samuel 15:11, it tells us that God is displeased:

> *"I regret that I have made Saul king, for he has turned back from following Me, and has not carried out My commands. And Samuel was distressed and cried out to the Lord all night."*

Saul's life went back and forth, saying he would follow God, but never giving his full heart to God and never sacrificing for Him. He says he transgresses against the Lord many times and that he will follow Him, but always falls. There was no peace in the land and God chose another man to be king. In chapter 16, the Lord tells Samuel in verse 1,

> *"How long will you grieve over Saul, since I have rejected him from being king over Israel? Fill your horn with oil, and go; I will send to you Jesse the Bethlehemite, for I have selected a king for Myself among his sons."*

So Samuel goes to Bethlehem to meet the sons of Jesse. Samuel takes particular notice of Jesse's eldest son. But in verse 7,

> *"... the Lord said to Samuel, 'Do not look at his appearance or at the height of his stature, because I have rejected him; for God sees not as man sees, for man looks at the outward appearance, but the Lord looks at the heart."*

So Jesse parades all of his sons before Samuel and Samuel says to him in verse 11,

> *"... 'are these all your children?' And he said, 'There remains yet the youngest, and behold, he is tending the sheep.' Then Samuel said to Jesse, 'Send and bring him; for we will not sit down until he comes here.'"*

You see, God had a plan. A big plan. It would go down in history as one of the most well-known stories of all time. Then in verses 12-13 it reads,

"So he sent and brought him in. Now he was ruddy, with beautiful eyes and a handsome appearance. And the Lord said, 'Arise, anoint him; for this is he.' Then Samuel took the horn of oil and anointed him in the midst of his brothers; and the Spirit of the Lord came mightily upon David from that day forward. And Samuel arose and went to Ramah."

Evil spirits come upon Saul, and David is sent to play his harp for him. David was a skilled musician. When he played his harp, the spirits departed. Saul loved David for his musical ability, but it eventually turned to resentment.

The Philistines were a mighty army and were continually against Israel. In chapter 17, the Philistines had gathered and were on the mountain on one side and Israel was on the other. Then Goliath, their champion, comes out, a true giant over nine feet tall. He had a bronze helmet on his head and was clothed with full-scale armor made of bronze. He had a bronze javelin slung between his shoulders. His spear was made of iron, and he had a shield bearer with him. He tells Israel to choose someone to fight with him. And he makes a deal. If the Israelite wins, then the Philistines will serve Israel, but if he loses, then Israel will serve the Philistines. So as you can imagine, there weren't a lot of people volunteering, and Saul and his army were afraid. For forty days, Goliath made the challenge. No one would fight him, then David hears of it. He had been off tending the sheep. David left his sheep to take provisions to his brothers at the Israelite camp. He hears Goliath's challenge and asks questions of the Israelite soldiers. Saul hears of it and sends for David. In 1 Samuel 17:32-37, it says,

"Then David said to Saul, 'Let no man's heart fail on account of him; your servant will go and fight with this Philistine. Then Saul said to David, 'You are not able to go against this Philistine; for you are but a youth while he has been a warrior from his youth.' But David said to Saul, 'Your servant was tending his father's sheep. When a lion or bear came and took a lamb from the flock, I went out after him and attacked him, and rescued it from his mouth; and when he rose up against me, I seized him by his beard and struck him and killed him. Your servant has killed both lion and bear; and this uncircumcised Philistine will be like one of them, since he has taunted the armies of the living God.' And David said, 'The Lord who delivered me from the paw of the lion and the paw of the bear, He will deliver me from the hand of the Philistine.'"

David accepts the challenge. He does not even flinch. He speaks with such confidence knowing that his mighty and powerful God will deliver him. Saul and his men give David armor and weapons, but David does not want them because he has never used them before and he knows in his heart of hearts God will protect him. David has a strong faith in God to deliver him. So he gathers five smooth stones and puts them in his pouch, grabs his sling in his hand, and approaches the Philistine. The Bible tells us that Goliath looks at David with disdain. He says to David in verse 43,

"Am I a dog, that you come at me with sticks?

David responds in verses 45-49,

> *"Then David said to the Philistine, 'You come to me with a sword, a spear and a javelin, but I come to you in the name of the Lord of hosts, The God of the armies of Israel, whom you have taunted. This day the Lord will deliver you up into my hands, and I will strike you down and remove your head from you. And I will give the dead bodies of the army of the Philistines this day to the birds of the sky and the wild beasts of the earth, that all the earth may know that there is a God in Israel, and that all this assembly may know that the Lord does not deliver by sword or by spear; for the battle is the Lord's and He will give you into our hands.' Then it happened when the Philistine rose and came and drew near to meet David, that David ran quickly toward the battle line to meet the Philistine. And David put his hand into his bag and took from it a stone and slung it, and struck the Philistine on his forehead. And the stone sank into his forehead, so that he fell on his face to the ground."*

No fear. No pausing. Just boldness to do what he knew he had to do to save Israel and confidence that God would deliver him. David fought to bring glory to God. God would be triumphant.

This is just the beginning of David's story in the Bible. David is just a brave young lad, but he becomes king. Word gets out across the land about David that he slew the giant and protected their country. Even Saul's son Jonathan loves David. Saul becomes resentful. After all, he is the current king. David is chased by Saul for years in the desert.

One of the most memorable scenes from the times in the desert is when David and his men are hiding and Saul is in a nearby cave. Some of his men come to David and tell him in 1 Samuel 24:4,

> "... 'This is the day of which the Lord said to you, 'Behold, I will deliver your enemy into your hand, that you may do to him as it seems good to you.' And David arose and secretly cut off a corner of Saul's robe."

And although David could have done more harm to Saul than just damaging his robe, his conscience still troubles him. David knew God placed Saul as king. David humbly runs out of the cave and calls out to Saul in verses 8-10,

> "... saying, 'My lord and my king!' And when Saul looked behind him, David stooped with his face to the earth, and bowed down. And David said to Saul, 'Why do you listen to the words of men who say, Indeed David seeks you harm? Look, this day your eyes have seen that the Lord delivered you today into my hand in the cave, and someone urged me to kill you, and I said, 'I will not stretch out my hand against my lord, for he is the Lord's anointed."

Saul then knows that David is more righteous than he. And although this sparring goes on much longer, we can see that David continues to be bold for God. Saul could have killed David when David came out of the cave, but God honored his faithfulness.

There are dozens more passages about David. I cannot share them all here, but I want you to know that although King David eventually sins and receives the painful consequences, he continues to serve God.

I remember as a young believer thinking, "How is David a man after God's own heart if he continually sins"? But through the years, I have learned that a willing and a contrite heart are precious to God. Over and over in the book of Psalms, David cries out to God. His heart is broken, but he never fails in his trust in who God is or that God will provide for him and comfort him. And he ends many psalms with praise, no matter what has happened.

Here are some of my favorite verses from the Psalms.

Psalm 4:1, 8 - Answer me when I call, O God of my righteousness! Thou hast relieved me in my distress; Be gracious to me and hear my prayer.

In peace I will both lie down and sleep, for thou alone, O Lord, dost make me to dwell in safety.

Psalm 6:1-2, 6, 8-9 - O Lord, do not rebuke me in Thine anger, nor chasten me in Thy wrath. Be gracious to me, O Lord, for I am pining away; Heal me, O Lord, for my bones are dismayed.

I am weary with my sighing; Every night I make my bed swim, I dissolve my couch with my tears.

Depart from me, all you who do iniquity, for the Lord has heard the voice of my weeping. The Lord has heard my supplication, The Lord receives my prayer.

Psalm 16:7-8 - I will bless the Lord who has counseled me; Indeed, my mind instructs me in the night. I have set the Lord continually before me; because he is at my right hand, I will not be shaken.

Psalm 22:1-2, 31 - My God, my God why hast thou forsaken me? Far from my deliverance are the words of my groaning. O my God, I cry by day, but Thou dost not answer; and by night, but I have no rest.

They will come and will declare His righteousness to a people who will be born, that He has performed it.

Psalm 34:17-18 -The righteous cry and the Lord hears, and delivers them out of all their troubles,

the Lord is near to the brokenhearted, and saves those who are crushed in spirit.

My Very Favorites

Psalm 37:23-24 - The steps of a man are established by the Lord; and He delights in his way, When he falls, he shall not be hurled headlong; Because the Lord is the One who holds his hand.

Psalm 51:10-12, 17 - Create in me a clean heart, O God, and renew a steadfast spirit within me. Do not cast me away from Thy presence, and do not take Thy Holy Spirit from me.

Restore to me the joy of Thy salvation, and sustain me with a willing spirit.

The sacrifices of God are a broken spirit; a broken and a contrite heart, O God, Thou wilt not despise.

Psalm 63:7 - For Thou hast been my help, and in the shadow of Thy wings I sing for joy.

WHAT IS YOUR FAVORITE

VERSE IN THE BOOK OF PSALMS?

The book of Psalms has always been a favorite of mine. Going through much heartache as a young person, I clung to them because David's emotions were raw and he was honest with God. He would yell at God in confusion or cry with pain. He does not hold anything back. I believe this is why God loves him so, because his heart is laid bare and he never loses faith or trust in God.

... AND THE WOMAN WAS INTELLIGENT AND BEAUTIFUL IN APPEARANCE...THEN DAVID SAID TO ABIGAIL, "BLESSED BE THE LORD GOD OF ISRAEL, WHO SENT YOU THIS DAY TO MEET ME, AND BLESSED BE YOUR DISCERNMENT...."
I SAMUEL 25:3 & 32-33

CHAPTER 25

Abigail

Woman of Wisdom and Discernment

Several years ago, I was reading along in I Samuel and read about Abigail. I was amazed at her insight, resourcefulness, ingenuity, and boldness as she saved her people from harm. It is not one of the foremost stories you often think about, but has become a favorite of mine. I think maybe because it demonstrates to us how we can make things happen quickly if need be. The human spirit is resilient, and God can give us the wisdom and discernment to know what to do when there's a problem.

David and his men were watching over Nabal's sheep in the wilderness. Abigail was married to Nabal. She was intelligent and beautiful. The name Nabal means "fool," which is an appropriate name for this man. Abigail means "My father is joy." Nabal was living in Caleb's tribal holdings. He was a descendant of Caleb. However, he did not follow in Caleb's spiritual footsteps.

Nabal has a feast to celebrate the shearing of the sheep. David hears that Nabal is nearby and sends his men to collect payment for protecting

Nabal's sheep. David's men were totally rebuffed by Nabal and he did not pay David's men. Obviously, this did not please David. Everyone knew that David would become king and was God's choice. It was a foolish decision on Nabal's part.

Abigail moves quickly into action. She knows her husband has acted wrongly and also knows that David will most likely retaliate. She realizes Nabal will not approve, but knows that David is God's choice for king. She chooses to obey God.

And she is right. David swears he will kill every male in Nabal's household. Abigail prepares. In 1 Samuel 25:18-19 it says,

> *"Then Abigail hurried and took two hundred loaves of bread and two jugs of wine and five sheep already prepared and five measures of roasted grain and a hundred cakes of figs, and loaded them on donkeys. And she said to her young men, 'Go on before me; behold, I am coming after you.' But she did not tell her husband Nabal."*

Not only does Abigail not want harm to come to her people, but she does not want David to seek revenge and ruin his reputation as the future God-chosen king of Israel. I think this is amazing. She seeks the good for everyone. And she moves quickly and has a great plan to ward off the crises.

When Abigail sees David on the road coming toward her, she dismounts her donkey and falls on her face before David. She says to him in verses 24-28,

"And she fell to his feet and said, 'On me alone, my lord, be the blame. And please let your maidservant speak to you, and listen to the words of your maidservant. Please do not let my lord pay attention to this worthless man, Nabal, for as his name and folly is with him; but I your maidservant did not see the young men of my lord whom you sent. Now therefore, my lord, as the Lord lives, and as your soul lives, since the Lord has restrained you from shedding blood, and from avenging yourself by your own hand, now then let your enemies, and those who seek evil against my lord, be as Nabal. And now let this gift which your maidservant has brought to my lord be given to the young men who accompany my lord. Please forgive the transgression of your maidservant; for the Lord will certainly make for my lord an enduring house, because my lord is fighting the battles of the Lord, and evil shall not be found in you all your days."

Wow. Not only beautiful, but brilliant. David was probably stunned at such a speech. She also takes the blame for not knowing David's men were met harshly by Nabal. She continues to tell him he will be ruler over Israel, and to remember her. Then David responds to Abigail in verses 32-33,

"... 'Blessed be the Lord God of Israel, who sent you this day to meet me, and blessed be your discernment, and blessed be you, who have kept me this day from bloodshed, and from avenging myself from my own hand."

He takes the goods she has prepared for him and his men and returns home. Nabal is still partying, and so she decides not to tell him until morning what has happened. In the morning, when she reports to Nabal, his heart dies within him and ten days later, he dies. David hears of this and sends a proposal of marriage to Abigail.

When I read this story, not only do I think Abigail is bold and quick-thinking, but I also think she acts wisely and is quite discerning. I am also amazed at her ability to pull all her resources together quickly in a time of crisis. I realize Nabal was wealthy and she had ways to gather a great amount of goods with the help of servants. We do not all have the means nor ability to do something like this on a large scale. However, this story is so inspiring to me. If I had an immediate tragedy, would I be able to think quickly to come to someone's aid, would I be able to pull resources together, and would the other person feel blessed by it?

Wisdom and discernment do not come to us overnight, but over a long period of time. Praying for God to grow us in these traits is a great way to start. You can also pray for Him to give you opportunities to help others in big ways using these gifts of discernment and wisdom.

...THE KING SPOKE AND SAID TO DANIEL, "YOUR GOD WHOM YOU CONSTANTLY SERVE WILL HIMSELF DELIVER YOU."

DANIEL 6:16

CHAPTER 26

Daniel and His Faithful Friends

Standing Firm

WHEN I THINK OF OBEDIENCE TO GOD,

DANIEL COMES TO MIND IMMEDIATELY.

Daniel did not waver in his faith. He was rock solid. He made quite an impression on the king and those around him with his bold and purposeful actions. Sometimes when there are miraculous stories from scripture, they are taught to children, and as adults, we don't seem to focus on them. I mean, everyone has heard of Daniel and the lions' den. Don't get me wrong, children should hear of this miraculous story. But so should adults. It teaches us to stand up for our beliefs, no matter the consequences.

The book of Daniel is to the Old Testament what Revelation is to the New Testament. It covers the entire time period of the Babylonian captivity. Nine of the twelve chapters relate to prophecies given in dreams. Not only is there talk of future plans for Israel, but also current ones. The book begins in 605 B.C. when Babylon conquered Jerusalem. Daniel was taken from his homeland to Babylon with his three friends and many others.

Other prophets had forewarned Israel of what would happen because of their unbelief. Israel's exile resulted from their disobedience to God. God did not fail His people, but in His sovereignty, He allowed Israel to suffer so that they would see God's power in the coming Messiah as king. The book of Daniel was written to encourage those exiled Jews, telling them of God's promises for them.

There were many miracles in Daniel. God used miracles and prophetic dreams to demonstrate His sovereignty and reveal His power.

The Babylonian leaders of the time chose and trained some of the captives to be leaders so they would eventually be able to help Babylon take over more countries. Usually the men were young, most likely in their teens. They would choose ones who were 1) physically free from bodily blemish and handsome, 2) mentally sharp, and 3) poised and polished socially. They would be trained for three years. They also changed their names. Daniel, which means "God is my judge," was changed to Belteshazzar; Hananiah, "the Lord is gracious," was changed to Shadrach; Mishael, "who is like the Lord," was changed to Meshach; and Azariah, "the Lord is my helper" was changed to Abednego.

The four men were told to eat a specific diet which had been sacrificed to idols. They knew this was wrong, and it says in Daniel 1:8-10:

> *"But Daniel made up his mind that he would not defile himself with the king's choice food or with the wine which he drank; so he sought permission from the commander of the officials that he might not defile himself. Now God granted Daniel favor and compas-*

sion in the sight of the commander of the officials, and the commander of the officials said to Daniel, 'I am afraid of my lord the king, who has appointed your food and your drink; for why should he see your faces looking more haggard than the youths who are your own age? Then you would make me forfeit my head to the king.'"

By eating the king's food, Daniel knew it would be honoring the Babylonian deities. So Daniel asks for a trial for ten days. He and his friends will eat as they see fit. They ate vegetables, which may have included wheat or barley. Not only did God honor these actions, but they gained respect for their actions. At the end of the ten days, Daniel and his friends were in better health than the other young men. As a matter of fact, the king found them ten times better.

King Nebuchadnezzar had a very disturbing dream which none of his advisors could interpret. The king asks if Daniel could interpret. Daniel was careful to reply, but prays for God to give him the answer. God gives Daniel the answer and Daniel shares it with the king. King Nebuchadnezzar is so impressed and thankful. He tells Daniel that surely Daniel's God is the God of gods and a Lord of kings and a revealer of mysteries. King Nebuchadnezzar promoted Daniel as ruler over Babylon. He made Shadrach, Meshach, and Abednego leaders over the administration, and Daniel was to serve in the court.

Even though King Nebuchadnezzar was impressed with Daniel's God for interpreting his dream, the king made a golden image that resembled the image from the dream. Then the king made a decree that whenever the people of the land saw the image, they must bow down and worship the image, and whoever did not bow down would be cast into a burn-ing furnace. So of course, Shadrach, Meshach, and Abednego did not fall on their knees to worship the statue. The king's men tell him of this. The three did not mean to disrespect the king, but once again, they could not worship an idol. They tell this to the king. The king was furious and asked for the heat to be turned up seven times hotter than normal. The three men are put into the furnace. Because the fire was so hot, the heat actually burned to death the men putting Shadrach, Meshach, and Abednego into the furnace. In Daniel 3:24-25, it tells us,

> *"Then Nebuchadnezzar the king was astounded and stood up in haste; he responded and said to his high officials, 'Was it not three men we cast bound into the midst of the fire?' They answered and said to the king, 'Certainly, O king.' He answered and said, 'Look! I see four men loosed and walking about in the midst of the fire without harm, and the appearance of the fourth is like a son of the gods!'"*

The king asks them to come out. The three men came out and were not harmed. Their hair was not singed, nor their clothing destroyed. Ne-buchadnezzar tells everyone that an angel from the God the three men worshipped protected them, and announces that no one is to say anything against their God. The king tells all the people that their God is the only one who could do such a thing, and Shadrach, Meshach, and Abednego prospered in the province of Babylon.

Toward the end of his life, Nebuchadnezzar again acknowledges the God of Daniel and his friends in 4:1-3:

"Nebuchadnezzar the king to all the peoples, nations and men of every language that live in all the earth: 'May your peace abound! It has seemed good to me to declare the signs and wonders which the Most High God has done for me. How great are His signs, and how mighty are His wonders! His kingdom is an everlasting kingdom, and His dominion is from generation to generation.'"

Then, after years of serving Nebuchadnezzar, his son Belshazzar, and then King Darius, Daniel had risen to great esteem. He had interpreted many dreams and always stood by his convictions. The kingdom of Babylon had been given over to the Medes and Persians. And Daniel had been made one of the commissioners. King Darius had planned on appointing him over the entire kingdom. Other leaders were not happy about this and began trying to find a ground for accusation against Daniel. No corruption was found in him, so they decided the best course of action was to establish a statute that they knew would go against Daniel's convictions. Daniel 6:7-9 states,

"All the commissioners of the kingdom, the prefects and the satraps, the high officials and the governors have consulted together that the king should establish a statute and enforce an injunction that anyone who makes a petition to any god or man besides you, O king, for thirty days, shall be cast into the lions' den. Now, O king establish the injunction and sign the document so that it may not be changed, according to the law of the Medes and Persians, which may not be

The Medo-Persian Empire was vast and encompassed parts of modern-day Greece, Turkey, Egypt, the Middle East, Iraq, Iran, and reached as far as India. It was larger than any previous empire in history, including the Babylonian Empire it had conquered circa 539 B.C. The events recorded in the book of Esther occurred after the end of the seventy-year Jewish captivity in Babylon, and before the rebuilding of the Temple in Jerusalem led by Ezra.

Esther, like the book of Exodus, shows how a foreign power tried to eliminate the Jewish race and how God preserved His people.

The book of Esther begins in the third year of the reign of the Persian king Ahasuerus. This name is equivalent to Xerxes, and Ahasuerus is usually identified in modern sources as Xerxes. The Greek Septuagint and classical sources identify him as Artaxerxes or Artaxerxes II.

The word "banquet" is in this book twenty-four times. The theme surrounds a very sudden turn of events: the Jews are destined to be destroyed, but instead are saved. The power of God is at work behind these extraordinary events, even though the name of God is not contained within the book.

King Ahasuerus, ruler of the Persian Empire, holds a lavish 180-day banquet, initially for his court and dignitaries and afterward a seven-day banquet for all the inhabitants of the capital city. On the seventh day of the banquet, the king orders the queen, Vashti, to display her beauty by coming to see the guests at the banquet wearing her crown. She refuses, infuriating the king. He takes the advice of his counselors to remove her from her position as an example to other women who may disobey their husbands.

> *"On the seventh day, when the heart of the king was merry with wine, he commanded Mehuman, Biztha, Harbona, Bigtha, Abagtha, Zethar, and Carkas*

the seven eunuchs who served in the presence of King Ahasuerus, to bring Queen Vashti before the king with her royal crown in order to display her beauty to the people and the princes, for she was beautiful. But Queen Vashti refused to come at the king's command delivered by the eunuchs. Then the king became very angry and his wrath burned within him. Then the king said to the wise men who understood the times—for it was the custom of the king so to speak before all who knew the law and justice, and were close to him; Carshena, Shethaar, Admantha, Tarshish, Meres, Marsena, and Memucan, the seven princes of Persia and Media who had access to the king's presence and sat in the first place in the kingdom—'According to the law, what is to be done with Queen Vashti, because she did not obey the command of King Ahasuerus delivered by the eunuchs?' And in the presence of the king and princes, Memucan said, 'Queen Vashti has wronged not only the king but also all the princes, and all the people who are in all the provinces of King Ahasuerus. For the queen's conduct will become known to all the women causing them to look in contempt on their husbands saying, 'King Ahashuerus commanded Queen Vashti to be brought into his presence, but she did not come.' And this day the ladies of Persia and Media who have heard of the queen's conduct will speak in the same way to all the king's princes, and there will be plenty of contempt and anger. If it pleases the king, let a royal edict be issued by him and let it be written in the laws of Persia and Media so that it cannot be repealed, that Vashti should come no more to King Ahaseurus, and let the king give her royal position to another who is more worthy than she.'"

ESTHER 1:10-19

A decree follows that

"every man should bear rule in his own house."

ESTHER 1:20-22

Ahasuerus then makes arrangements to choose a new queen from a selection of beautiful young women from throughout the empire.

"After these things when the anger of King Ahasuerus had subsided, he remembered Vashti and what she had done and what had been decreed against her. Then the king's attendants, who served him, said, 'Let the beautiful young virgins be sought for the king, And let the king appoint overseers in all the provinces of the kingdom that they may gather every beautiful young virgin to Susa the capital, to the harem, into the custody of Hegai, the king's eunuch, who was in charge of the women; and let their cosmetics be given them. Then let the young lady who pleases the king be queen in place of Vashti.' And the matter pleased the king, and he did accordingly."

ESTHER 2:1-4

Among these women is an orphaned Jewish woman named Esther. Through a series of events, she finds favor in the king's eyes and is crowned queen. At about the same time, Mordecai discovers a plot to assassinate the king. The conspirators are apprehended and hanged, and Mordecai's deed is recorded.

After a few years, King Ahasuerus appoints Haman, a descendant of the Amalekite people, to be his second-in-command. Mordecai falls into Haman's disfavor for refusing to bow down to him. (3:2-5). Haman is informed that Mordecai refuses to pay homage to him because Mordecai is Jewish.

Mordecai and Haman, in this book, have not forgotten their ancestral feud that goes back 550 years. Enmity between God's chosen people and the Amalekites began right after the Israelites left Egypt for the Promised Land (Exodus 17:8-16). The Amalekites attacked the Israelites, and because of this God declared that the Amalekites were to be wiped out.

> *"Remember what Amalek did to you along the way when you came out from Egypt, how he met you along the way and attacked among you all the stragglers at your rear when you were faint and weary; and he did not fear God."*
>
> DEUTERONOMY 25:17-19

It seems that Haman inherited his hatred of the Jewish people, as he forms a plot to kill not just Mordecai, but all Jews in the entire kingdom. He was given carte blanche from Ahasuerus to destroy an unnamed people group who were "different" than others in the kingdom. Lots had been cast to choose a date for the day of destruction, and a royal decree was issued throughout the kingdom to kill all Jews on that date.

> *"And letters were sent by couriers to all the king's provinces to destroy, to kill and annihilate all the Jews, both young and old, women and children, in one day, the thirteenth day of the twelfth month, which is the month of Adar, and to seize their possessions as plunder. A copy of the edict to be issued as law in every province was published to all the peoples so that they should be ready for this day. The couriers went out impelled by the king's command while the decree was issued in Susa the capital; and while the king and Haman sat down to drink, the city of Susa was in confusion."*

DEUTERONOMY 3:13-15

When Mordecai hears of this decree, he goes into mourning and asks Queen Esther to intercede with the King.

> *"When Mordecai learned all that had been done, he tore his clothes, put on sackcloth and ashes, and went out into the midst of the city and wailed loudly and bitterly. And went as far as the king's gate, for no one was to enter the king's gate clothed in sackcloth. And in each and every province where the command and decree of the king came, there was great mourning among the Jews, with fasting, weeping, and wailing; and many lay on sackcloth and ashes. Then Esther's maidens and her eunuchs came and told her, and the queen writhed in great anguish. And she sent garments*

to clothe Mordecai that he might remove his sackcloth from him, but he did not accept them." (4:1-4)

ESTHER 4:1-4

But she is afraid to go to the king unsummoned, which is punishable by death. So she creates a plan. She directs all the Jews in Susa to fast for three days, herself included. On the third day, she goes before King Ahasuerus. He stretches out his sceptre to her to indicate that she is not to be punished for appearing without an invitation. Esther does not request anything of the King, but invites him and Haman to a feast she prepared. During the feast, she again does not tell the King what she has on her mind; she asks them to attend another feast the next evening. Meanwhile, Haman is again offended when he sees Mordecai outside the palace, and at his wife's and friends' suggestion, has gallows built to have Mordecai hanged the next morning.

ESTHER 5:9-14

That night, Ahasuerus cannot sleep, and orders the court records to be read to him. He is reminded that Mordecai never received any recognition for revealing the plot against the king's life. Just then, Haman arrives, and the king asks what is to be done for a man the king wishes to honor. Haman thinks he is the one the king wants to honor, but to his horror, it is Mordecai who receives the honors.

WHEN ELIZABETH HEARD MARY'S GREETING,
THE BABY LEAPED IN HER WOMB; AND
ELIZABETH WAS FILLED WITH THE HOLY SPIRIT,
AND SHE CRIED OUT WITH A LOUD VOICE AND
SAID, "BLESSED ARE YOU AMONG WOMEN, AND
BLESSED IS THE FRUIT OF YOUR WOMB!"
LUKE 1:41-42

CHAPTER 28

Mary

A Special Calling

There are many Marys in the New Testament, but that cannot overshadow the importance of the mother of Jesus. The virgin birth is a great fundamental doctrine of our faith. If there is no virgin birth, we have no belief in Jesus as the Son of God. But I think the part that always grabs my heart is that Mary was so very young and was engaged to someone. How she must have had all sorts of questions in her mind. And truthfully, she must have been very scared.

Mary was actually called Miriam, after the sister of Moses. Miriam is Hebrew, while Mary is a New Testament blend of two Greek names: Mariam and Maria. Mary was faithful and courageous. In Isaiah 7:14, it tells us,

"Therefore the Lord Himself will give you a sign: The virgin will conceive and give birth to a son, and will call him Immanuel."

⁘

Mary was a peasant, which included skilled tradespeople. Mary most likely spent most of her time doing household chores for the clusters of families around the courtyard where she lived. It is estimated that she would have been about thirteen years of age, as that is about the age young women would become engaged in that era. She had been taught about the Messiah her entire life, and as a Jew, she would have accepted this announcement as part of God's plan.

"And coming in, he said to her, 'Hail, favored one! The Lord is with you.' But she was greatly troubled at this statement, and kept pondering what kind of salutation this might be. And the angel said to her, 'Do not be afraid, Mary; for you have found favor with God. And behold you will conceive in your womb, and bear a son, and you shall name Him Jesus. He will be great, and will be called the Son of the most High; and the Lord God will give Him the throne of His father David; and He will reign over the house of Jacob forever; and His kingdom will have no end.' And Mary said to the angel, 'How can this be, since I am a virgin?' and the angel answered and said to her, 'The Holy Spirit will come upon you, and the power of the Most High will overshadow you; and for that reason the holy offspring shall be called the Son of God. And behold, even your relative Elizabeth has also conceived a son in her old age; and she who was

called barren is now in her sixth month. For nothing is impossible with God.' And Mary said, 'Behold, the bondslave of the Lord; be it done to me according to your word.' And the angel departed from her."

LUKE 1:28-38

And what is the very best thing for her? To go to Elizabeth. Talk to an older woman, sing, pray, be counseled, and have time to think. These are great things. And Elizabeth is so excited to see her. What a joyful time that must have been.

Mary was the only person present at both Jesus' birth and His death.

"Therefore the soldiers did these things. But there were standing by the cross of Jesus, His mother, and His mother's sister, Mary the wife of Clopas, and Mary Magdalene. When Jesus therefore saw His mother, and the disciple whom He loved standing nearby, He said to His mother, 'Woman, behold your son!' Then He said to the disciple, 'Behold your mother!' And from that hour the disciple took her into his own household."

JOHN 19:25-27

We know from this passage that Jesus cared about His mother and wanted her to be taken care of by someone He knew and loved. I can't imagine how difficult it would be to watch your son die.

AND HE SAID TO THEM. "GO INTO ALL THE WORLD AND PREACH THE GOSPEL TO ALL CREATION..." AND THEY WENT OUT AND PREACHED EVERYWHERE....
MARK 16:15 & 20

CHAPTER 29

His Disciples

World Changers

The disciples were world changers. They did not know this at first. They were common men. Nothing fancy, not really leaders of any sort. Little did they know when they were chosen how their lives would change forever. They give us hope because they were like all of us, humanly flawed, but willing. And in three years' time, nothing would ever be the same. Jesus would call them to become the leaders of a movement like the world had never seen. Their influence would last forever. Let's take a look at these men Jesus chose to follow him.

> *"And it was at this time that He went off to the mountain to pray, and He spent the whole night in prayer to God. And when day came, He called His disciples to Him; and chose twelve of them, whom He also named as apostles: Simon, whom He also named Peter, and Andrew his brother; and James and John; and Philip and Bartholomew; and Matthew and*

Thomas; James the son of Alphaeus, and Simon who was called the Zealot; Judas the son of James, and Judas Iscariot, who became a traitor."

LUKE 6:12-16

A radical, a tax collector, fishermen, craftsmen, and tradesmen. They were mostly from the region of Galilee. They were personally chosen by Christ, and as common as they were, they would carry out the ministry, found the church, and all but one would be martyred for Christ's sake. They would heal the sick, cast out demons, and on the night of Jesus' betrayal, they would all abandon Him. (Matthew 26:56)

By the time they were chosen, Jesus already had a following. Why twelve? I am not sure. After Jesus' ascension, the apostles chose Mathias to fill the office vacated by Judas. But one thing is for certain. Jesus wanted all of us to know that anyone can follow Him. He had a strategy. Eleven of these men would teach and travel and build the church. All for the sake of the gospel.

The word *disciple* means "student" in Greek. And that is what they became. They would follow Jesus everywhere and learn from him. And in turn, others would learn from them.

"And they were continually devoting themselves to the apostles' teaching and to fellowship, to the breaking of bread and to prayer."

ACTS 2:42

All but one of these men shared the passion of telling others about Christ. They devoted their lives to it and triumphed in it against overwhelming opposition. They are fitting heroes and role models for us, despite their shortcomings. To study their lives is to get to know the men who were closest to Christ during His earthly life. To realize that they were ordinary people just like us is a great blessing.

> *"For I consider your calling, brethren, that there were not many wise according to the flesh, not many mighty, not many noble; but God has chosen the foolish things of the world to shame the wise, and God has chosen the weak things of the world to shame the things which are strong,"*

1 CORINTHIANS 1:26-27

Christ was going to use these men who did not seem mighty to show the world anyone could do the impossible. He encouraged them, spent time instructing them, and gave them special assignments. He also corrected them. They were always learning, though they did have a lack of spiritual understanding. What a refreshing reminder that He can use us too!

> *"And He said to them, 'O foolish men and slow of heart to believe in all that the prophets have spoken!"*

LUKE 24:25

They lacked faith (Matthew 6:30, 8:26) and they lacked commitment (Mark 14:50). But His strength is made perfect in weakness (2 Corinthians 12:9).

Here is a mini overview of the Twelve. As you read through it, try to determine which one you relate to the most.

Peter

(who had been Simon)

He is always listed first, which indicates he is their spokesman, their leader. He was the first to answer a question of Jesus. In Matthew 16:15-19, Jesus asks,

> *"But who do you say that I am? And Simon Peter answered and said, 'Thou art the Christ, the son of the living God'. And Jesus answered and said to him, 'Blessed are you Simon Barjona, because flesh and blood did not reveal this to you, but my Father who is in Heaven. And I say also to you Peter, and upon this rock I will build My church; and the gates of Hades shall not overpower it. I will give you the keys to the kingdom of heaven; and whatever you shall bind on earth shall be bound in heaven, and whatever you shall loose on earth shall be loosed in Heaven."*

Jesus renames him. Peter means "rock." Peter fails in many ways. He is impulsive and always boldly speaks out, sometimes in not the best of ways. However, he becomes the rock Jesus uses to build the church, and with all his blunders, he is the one who steps up to preach at Pentecost. We often think of him as the one who denies Jesus three times or impulsively cuts off the guard's ear, but there is nothing timid about Peter, and Christ knew

He had to have a leader who would not back down as His church would be built after His death. Peter's name is mentioned more times in the gospels than anyone, except Christ.

Keep in mind that the other disciples ran for their lives, and Peter was the only one who couldn't abandon Christ completely after he was arrested. He wanted to stay close to the Lord. Peter kept learning that Jesus still wanted to use him, no matter how many times he failed. This is such an encouragement to me, as I know I often fail. He wants to use all of us in different ways, but we can take this as a great lesson.

"Above all, keep fervent in your love for one another,
because love covers a multitude of sins."

1 PETER 4:8

Peter did learn how important love is because no matter how he fails, Jesus loves him so. Early church documents say that when it was Peter's time to be martyred, he asked to be crucified upside down because he was not worthy to die as his Lord had died. Peter's final words of his second epistle were: *"Grow in grace and in the knowledge of our Lord and Savior Jesus Christ."* (2 Peter 3:18) He was the greatest leader of the early church.

Andrew

Peter's brother is a fisherman by trade. Together, they were in charge of the family's fishing business. They were both from a small village called Bethsaida. Andrew was often in the background, but usually the one who introduced Jesus when they were in a group.

*"One of the two who heard John speak and fol-
lowed Him was Andrew, Simon Peter's brother. He
found first his own brother Simon, and said to him,
'We have found the Messiah'"*

JOHN 1:40-41

It is a wonderful thing that Andrew wanted to tell the person he loved most about Jesus and lead him to Christ.

Peter and Andrew had probably been lifelong companions with the other set of fishermen-brothers from Capernaum—James and John, sons of Zebedee. The four of them apparently shared common spiritual interests even before they met Christ. They had gone together to see John the Baptist. They are often referred to together. Together, they formed a collective leadership of the Twelve.

Andrew lived life in the spotlight of his outgoing brother. He did not seek to be in the limelight, but was content to be in the background and use his gifts for helping. He lived his whole life in the shadow of Peter, and he apparently accepted that role. This was the very thing that made him so useful. His willingness to be in the background gave him insight the other disciples may not have seen.

At the feeding of the five thousand, it was Andrew who brought the boy with the loaves and fishes to Christ.

*"There is a lad here who has five barley loaves and
two small fish, but what are these for so many people?"*

JOHN 6:9

Andrew knew that this was not enough to feed five thousand people, but also knew Christ would not have had them look for food unless He would provide. Nothing is impossible for Jesus.

It is wonderful to see the Andrews of the world, quietly helping, not expecting praise. I am thankful for those in my life who silently help. Years ago, I remember a man at our church who had passed away. About six months after his death, our pastor mentioned that there were so many unseen things he had done at church that no one knew about. Someone would ask why something at church hadn't been done and they realized that Bill had been doing it all along and no one was even aware of it. That is an amazing way to serve.

James

James was the eldest of the inner circle of the disciples, but is the least mentioned. James and John were most likely from a well-known family and that is why they are often given the recognition as the sons of Zebedee. They were bold and often fought over who would be the greatest and who would have a place next to Jesus. Always hoping for a better position. James would be the first of the Twelve killed for his faith in Christ.

> *Acts 12:1-3, "Now about that time Herod the king laid hands on some who belonged to the church, in order to mistreat them. And he had James, the brother of John, put to death with a sword. And when he saw it pleased the Jews, he proceeded to arrest Peter also."*

James was passionate and headstrong. He learned many lessons and became a man of sensitivity and grace. God used him. I think the thing to remember is that Jesus called all Twelve, and He knew James was needed in furthering the early church. We all have an important, yet very different role in God's kingdom. It can be frustrating when you don't know why God has placed you somewhere or whether you will be acknowledged, but the outcome will always be to edify Him. Trust in Him when you don't have the answers.

John

We hear so much about John in our Bibles. Besides Paul and Luke, he wrote more of the New Testament than anyone else. In his gospel, he writes about Christ, in 1, 2, and 3 John, he writes instructions to the church, and in Revelation, he writes about the visions God gave him about the future. He played a major role in the early church. He also lived the longest. John is the only disciple not martyred.

He and his brother, James, are usually mentioned together in scripture. John was often referred to as "the apostle Jesus loved." The theme of love is seen in his writings. He was ambitious and passionate, just like his brother. But as you see him mature through the years, you see how his weaknesses became his greatest strengths. Of all the writers in the New Testament, he is the most black and white. He wanted to uphold the truth. No gray areas. We are either in the light or in the dark, in sin or out of sin.

One important event for Peter, James, and John was that they were chosen to see the transfiguration. Christ took His most trusted companions to show them God in all His glory. They had been given a preview of what was to come. But even after showing them His glory, the men argued over who was greatest. But Jesus tells them they need to be a servant.

"But they kept silent, for on the way they had dis-
cussed with one another which of them was the great-
est. And sitting down, He called the twelve and said to
them, 'If anyone wants to be first, he shall be last of all
and servant of all.' And taking a child, He set before
them, and taking him in His arms, He said to them,
'Whoever receives one child like this in My name re-
ceives Me; and whoever receives Me does not receive
Me, but Him who sent Me.'"

MARK 9:34-37

God does not see our failures as final. The disciples may have fled the night of Jesus' betrayal, but they would suffer for His sake. This is a good example for us as we share our faith and boldly live for the gospel of Christ.

Another example from scripture I love regarding John was that he was told by Jesus to care for His mother. Several witnesses from Jerusalem say that John does not leave Mary until she dies. Jesus knew that the heart of John would follow through with that request. That same love for His savior was why, when they reclined at the Last Supper, John was leaning on Jesus because of the love in his heart for the Lord.

Philip

In the four biblical lists of the twelve apostles, the fifth name on every list is Philip. Philip in Greek means "lover of horses." He is from the same city as Andrew and Peter. There is good evidence that Philip, Nathanael, and Thomas were also fishermen. If all seven fishermen were from around the same area, they most likely knew each other. This shows what a close-knit group the disciples were, having been friends long before they became disciples. It was great that most of the disciples knew each other having been from the same region and many of the same profession. They had an easy camaraderie. Why Jesus would choose men who knew each other rather than find the most gifted from all over the country? I think it is a great example of how God can use anyone. He will draw people to Himself and teach them.

John is the only gospel that talks about Philip, maybe because John knew him. Philip is practical and detail oriented. He also had an evangelistic heart. After he first met Jesus, he quickly went and found Nathanael to tell him about Christ. It is believed he was also the person in charge of the funds they needed for food or where the food was to come from. In John 6:5, Jesus asks him how they will get food.

Philip was probably a concrete thinker and did not necessarily grasp who Jesus was. He was usually thinking about the practical aspects of everything. In the upper room, when Jesus is feeling a sense of heaviness in His heart, He explains to the disciples that He is God.

> *"If you had known Me, you would have known My Father also; and from now on you know Him and have seen Him."*

JOHN 14:7

But in verse 8, we read,

> *"Philip said to Him, 'Lord, show us the Father, and it is sufficient for us.'"*

Philip didn't understand. He had been hearing Jesus teach for three years, but being focused on the practical, he did not always see the big picture. But, Jesus uses the weak to build His church. One does not need to be perfect.

Nathanael

In all four lists of the Twelve, Nathanael is listed as Bartholomew. In the Gospel of John, he is always called Nathanael Bartholomew. Nathanael means "God has given." He came from Cana in Galilee where Jesus did His first miracle. Philip and Nathanael are close friends and are usually listed together. In John 1:45, it says that Philip found Nathanael, showing that they were close companions. When Philip found Nathanael, he says

"We have found Him of whom Moses in the law, and also the prophets, wrote."

JOHN 1:45

This shows that Philip knew this would be important to Nathanael. And the fact he mentions the Messiah shows that Nathanael knew the Old Testament. When Jesus sees Nathanael coming toward Him, he says in verse 47,

"Behold, an Israelite indeed, in whom is no deceit!"

His devotion to God was real. Jesus saw that his heart was sincere and his faith was real. He sounds amazed in his response to Jesus. In verse 48, Nathanael responds,

"How do You know me? And Jesus answered him, 'Before Philip called you, when you were under the fig tree I saw you."

Jesus wasn't actually physically present when Nathanael was under the fig tree; Nathanael knew that. He realized Jesus could see into his very heart. Jesus often referred to Nathaniel as devoted and an "Israelite indeed."

Jesus answered and said to him, 'Because I said to you, 'I saw you under the fig tree', do you believe? You will see greater things than these.' And He said to him, 'Most assuredly, I say to you, hereafter you shall see heaven open, and the angels of God ascending and descending upon the Son of Man.'"

JOHN 1:50-51

It was a wonderful thing for someone to trust so fully from the start.

I love John 1:49,

Nathanael answered and said to Him, "Rabbi, You are the Son of God! You are the King of Israel!"

Nathanael traveled to Persia and India to share the gospel. He was martyred like the others; however, it is uncertain if he was crucified or cast into the sea.

Matthew
(also called Levi)
and Thomas

No matter how often I study the disciples, it amazes me that they just left what they were doing and followed Jesus. Matthew and Thomas are no different. Will you and I be the same way when the time comes?

> *"As Jesus passed on from there, He saw a man named Matthew sitting at the tax office. And He said to him, 'Follow Me.' So he arose and followed Him."*

MATTHEW 9:9

Both of these men had notorious monikers put on them. Matthew was the sinful tax collector and Thomas was the doubter. Talk about negative labels. However, Jesus called them into His inner circle. Jesus saw the men He wanted for His purposes.

Matthew is fairly reserved, and although the book of Matthew is rather lengthy, he only mentions his own name twice. Tax collectors were very despised people. They were the lowest of the low. They extorted money from people to pay Rome and took the extra for themselves. Matthew does not share much about himself; however, we know that he has a banquet in Jesus' honor and invites all sorts of sinful people. He wanted to introduce Jesus to all his friends. In Luke's gospel, we are told,

> *"Then Levi gave Him a great feast in his own house. And there were a great number of tax collectors*

and others who sat down with them. And the scribes and the Pharisees complained against His disciples, saying, 'Why do You eat and drink with tax collectors and sinners?' Jesus answered and said to them, 'Those who are well have no need of a physician, but those who are sick. I have not come to call the righteous, but sinners to repentance'"

LUKE 5:29-32

The only friends Matthew had were bad people, so it was quite the group, and the Pharisees were not happy about it. Matthew was a Jew and knew his Old Testament. His gospel quotes the Old Testament ninety-nine times. He was looking for the Messiah. It is not surprising that he dropped everything to follow Jesus.

Matthew was burned at the stake. He walked away from his money-making job and gave his all for Christ.

Thomas is often called Didymus, which means "twin." He apparently had a twin brother or sister. He is only mentioned once in each synoptic gospel, but more often in John's gospel. He seemed to anticipate the worst and was the questioner of the bunch.

However, when Lazarus dies and the other disciples do not want to travel back to Jerusalem, Thomas speaks up.

"Then Thomas, who is called Twin, said to his fellow disciples, 'Let us also go, that we may die with Him.'"

JOHN 11:16

The other disciples knew they were in danger if they went, and although Thomas also knows this, he was determined to be courageous and to die with Jesus. He was loyal. He was devoted to Christ. He did not want to live if Jesus was going to die.

In John 14:2-6, Jesus is telling them of the events in the near future. *"'In my Father's house are many dwelling places; if it were not so, I would have told you; for I go to prepare a place for you. And if I go to prepare a place for you, I will come again, and receive you unto Myself; that where I am, there you may be also. And you know the way where I am going.' And Thomas said to Him, 'Lord, we do not know where You are going, how do we know the way?' Jesus said to him, I am the way, and the truth, and the life; no one comes to the Father, but through Me.'"*

Thomas does not want to be left behind.

The most memorable scene for Thomas is where he derives his nickname, "doubting Thomas." Jesus had died. The disciples were discouraged that Jesus was gone. They gathered for comfort and safety. They sealed the windows and doors. All were there, except for Thomas. Suddenly, Jesus appears before them. They were glad when they saw the Lord. But Thomas was not there. He may have been so discouraged he wanted to go off on his own and process the fact he would not see Jesus again. He loved Jesus, and now He was gone and it broke his heart. The disciples found Thomas and told him the good news.

> *"The other disciples therefore were saying to him, 'We have seen the Lord!' But he said to them, 'Unless I shall see in His hands the imprint of the nails, and put my finger into the place of the nails, and*

put my hand into His side, I will not believe.' And after eight days again His disciples were inside, and Thomas was with them. Jesus came, the doors having been shut, and stood in their midst, and said, 'Peace be with you.' Then He said to Thomas, 'Reach here your finger, and see My hands; and reach here your hand and put into my side; and be not unbelieving, but believing.' Thomas answered and said to Him, 'My Lord and my God.' And Jesus said to him, 'Because you have seen Me, you have believed? Blessed are they who did not see, and yet believed.'"

JOHN 20:25-29

Keep in mind the other disciples also were mourning the loss of Jesus until they saw Him. Thomas was dealing with his grief in his own melancholy way. Thomas was in deep despair. Jesus was tender with him.

Thomas ended up also telling others about Christ, and there are landmarks in India documenting Thomas having a ministry there. Most extra- biblical writings have Thomas dying as a martyr from being run through with a spear.

These two men, Matthew, the chief sinner, and Thomas, not always the optimist, were transformed the same way the others were. Christ showed no partiality. He loved them all. He looked past their sins. Thank goodness for this. We have a Saviour who loves us no matter what we have done or been through. Grace is for us all if we trust in Him.

James – The Less; Simon – The Zealot; and Judas

(not Iscariot)

These men were not mentioned as much and so we do not know that much about them. They were called; they left their jobs and families to follow Christ. They are rarely in the foreground, but do end up sharing Christ with others and help establish the early church. Many others had been following Jesus at the beginning, but left after they saw how difficult it would be. These men stayed the course. Jesus loved using ordinary people in amazing ways. These men were living proof of that.

Judas

The Traitor

We cannot mention the disciples without mentioning Judas. He has gone down in history as the most evil disciple and a betrayer. He spent three years with Jesus, but for all that time, his heart was only growing hard.

He decided to follow Jesus, but never gave Him his heart. Jesus knew this when He chose him to follow him. It had been prophesied.

> *"I do not speak of all of you. I know the ones I have chosen; but it is that the Scripture may be fulfilled, He who eats My bread has lifted up his heel against Me."*

> JOHN 13:18

God ordained that Jesus would die. Judas made a choice to carry out this evil deed. Judas followed Jesus for his own gain. He never really loved Christ. He had an opportunity. He had heard every sermon the other disciples had heard. He never let on to the others and kept it hidden that he did not believe.

We see his frustration in Bethany when Mary pours out the costly perfume on Jesus' feet.

> *"But Judas Iscariot, one of His disciples, who was intending to betray Him, said, 'Why was this perfume not sold for three hundred denarii, and given to poor people?'"*

JOHN 12:4-5

It probably really bothered him to see the perfume go to waste. Judas resented Jesus. This was the last straw for Judas because he immediately goes out to talk to the chief priests.

> *"Then one of the twelve, named Judas Iscariot, went to the chief priests, and said, 'What are you willing to give me to deliver Him up to you? And they weighed out to him thirty pieces of silver. And from then on he began looking for a good opportunity to betray Him."*

MATTHEW 26:14-16

Judas comes back and sorta blends in, keeping a low profile. But Jesus knew what had transpired. In verse 21, Jesus says,

"Truly I say to you that one of you will betray Me."

Judas leaves, and they all go to the garden of Gethsemane.

> *"And while He was still speaking, behold, Judas, one of the twelve came up, accompanied by a great multitude with swords and clubs, from the chief priests and elders of the people. Now he who was betraying Him gave them a sign, saying, 'Whomever I shall kiss, He is the one; seize Him.' And immediately he went to Jesus and said, 'Hail, Rabbi!' and kissed Him. And Jesus said to him, 'Friend, do what you have come for.'"*

MATTHEW 26:47-50

Judas using a kiss was so devious. It made the act of betrayal even worse than it already was. Then Jesus called him friend. Ever gracious.

Afterward, Judas had to deal with his conscience. Matthew 27:3-4 says,

> *"Then Judas, His betrayer, seeing that He had been condemned, was remorseful and brought back the thirty pieces of silver to the chief priests and elders saying, 'I have sinned by betraying innocent blood.'"*

He left and went and hanged himself. Just because he felt remorseful does not mean he was repentant. He did not repent or seek forgiveness from God, he just felt terrible about his choices and decided to take away his pain. He was not bold for the cause of the gospel, and he did not serve God.

Matthias is later chosen to fill the place of Judas. He becomes a witness of Jesus' resurrection. A perfect example of another ordinary man who the Lord loved and elevated to an extraordinary calling.

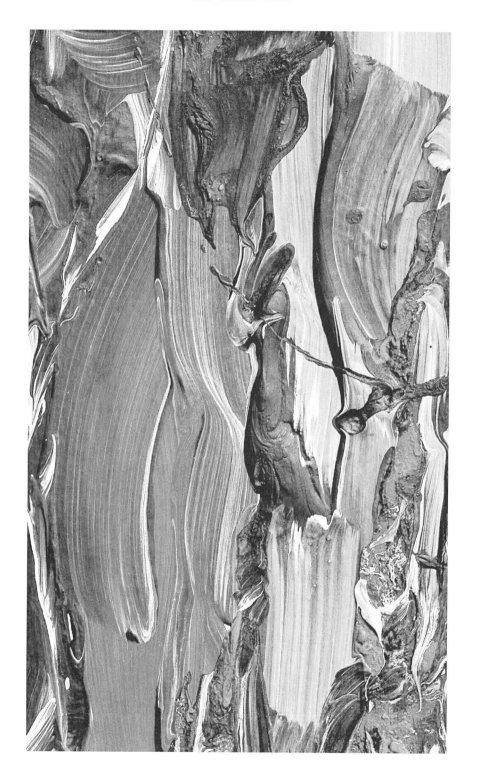

"AND I SAID, 'WHO ART THOU, LORD?' AND THE LORD SAID, 'I AM JESUS WHOM YOU ARE PERSECUTING. BUT ARISE, AND STAND ON YOUR FEET; FOR THIS PURPOSE I HAVE APPEARED TO YOU, TO APPOINT YOU A MINISTER AND A WITNESS ... TO OPEN THEIR EYES SO THAT THEY MAY TURN FROM DARKNESS TO LIGHT... IN ORDER THAT THEY MAY RECEIVE FORGIVENESS OF SINS AND AN INHERITANCE AMONG THOSE WHO HAVE BEEN SANCTIFIED BY FAITH IN ME.'

ACTS 26: 15-18"

CHAPTER 30

Paul

Spreading the Gospel

Christians often feel as if they have to travel to faraway places on mission trips to truly be missionaries or serve others. Your mission field might be at home, or it might be in a foreign land.

Paul traveled to many cities on his missionary journeys. But Philippi was truly special. From the book of Philippians, we see a central theme of lasting and abiding joy. Chapter two instructs each one of us to pursue Christlikeness, as it is shown as the most important element in spiritual growth. Paul wants us to pursue this, but no matter what happens, whether we are imprisoned or martyred, the main thread in this letter is joy. But how does he get to this point? Let us take a look at Paul's life to see his path.

Paul, who had been named Saul after the first king of Israel, was a learned man. He was trained by Gamaliel, who was the best of the best.

Saul was also a Jew, a Pharisee, and a Roman citizen. He knew the law backward and forward, and had no patience for those who did not follow the law. He persecuted Christians and was well known for ravaging towns. The book of Acts tells of his conversion. Acts was written by Luke, who ended up becoming Paul's friend and traveling companion and a physician. (Colossians 4:14)

The conversion of Paul is in Acts 9:1-9,

> *"Now Saul, still breathing threats and murder against the disciples of the Lord, went to the high priest, and asked for letters from him to the synagogues of Damascus, so that if he found any belonging to the Way, both men and women, he might bring them bound to Jerusalem. And it came about that as he journeyed, he was approaching Damascus, and suddenly a light from heaven flashed around him; and he fell to the ground, and heard a voice saying to him, 'Saul, Saul, why are you persecuting Me?' And he said, 'Who art thou, Lord?' And He said, 'I am Jesus whom you are persecuting, but rise, and enter the city, and it shall be told to you what you must do.' And the men who traveled with him stood speechless, hearing the voice, but seeing no one. And Saul got up from the ground, and though his eyes were open, he could see nothing; and leading him by the hand, they brought him to Damascus. And he was three days without sight, and neither ate nor drank."*

This was the first of six visions to be seen by Paul, as recorded in Acts. After three days, his eyesight was restored and he was filled with the Spirit. The Spirit had already been active in Paul's life: convicting him of sin (John 16:9), convincing him of the Lordship of Christ (1 Corinthians 12:3), transforming him (Titus 3:5), and indwelling him permanently (I Corinthians 12:13). He was then filled with the Spirit and empowered for service. Saul received the Spirit without any apostles present because he was a Jew and because he was an apostle in his own right because Jesus personally chose him and commissioned him for service. (Romans 1:1)

Paul then does what God has told him to do—go to the very people he was persecuting and show them that God can change their life just as He had changed his. He spends the first eleven chapters in Romans explaining that everyone, no matter their heritage or their sin can know Christ. Paul knows the gospel has the power to change everyone, and his passion is that all people would come believe in the gospel and be saved to accept Christ. Without knowing the gospel and what it teaches, how can we tell others? How can we be bold for Christ? It must start with us truly knowing Him.

Paul embarked on three missionary journeys. He went from town to town. In some towns, he was not welcome. Sometimes, he was run out of town. This did not stop him. He continued on, no matter the consequences because bottom line, without Christ, we spend eternity in hell. Paul knew this and traveled on foot to as many places as he could. He had an urgency and boldness to share Christ as far and as wide as he could before his time here on Earth was done.

On his first journey in 47-48 AD, he traveled mainly with Barnabas to Cyprus and Galatia. On the second journey in 49-52 AD, he was with Silas in Asia Minor and Greece. He stayed in Corinth for about a year and a half. He also visited Jerusalem and Antioch. Then he began his third journey in 52 AD. He stayed in Ephesus and wrote letters to the believers in Galatia and Corinth. In 55-57AD, he traveled through Greece and a bit north, and he wrote the letter to the Romans. He returned to Jerusalem and was arrested and imprisoned from 57-59 AD. He then was taken to Rome, and while under house arrest, wrote letters to the Philippians, Ephesians, Colossians, and to Philemon around 62 to 64 AD. He also wrote to Timothy and Titus. While in Rome, he was martyred. Paul spent well over a year in the cities he preached to, living with the believers there and modeling a lifestyle of imitating Christ. Over the course of his life, Paul likely traveled well over ten thousand miles to spread the gospel.

On Paul's first missionary journey, he performed his first miracle. (Acts 13:10-12) He generally went to the synagogue first. Usually, the Jews there were not receptive, but many gentiles were. Those who opposed him often sought to stone him and Barnabas, but they were able to flee. In Lystra, people thought they were gods and wanted to worship them. They tried to convince them otherwise. Paul was stoned there and left for dead, but got up the next morning and continued on his way.

Paul's second missionary journey is documented in Acts 15:36-18:22. He and his companions went back to see some of the churches they had started on the first journey. They met a believer on this journey named Timothy who became one of Paul's dearest companions. They wound their way through Asia (modern-day Turkey) and eventually ended up in Philippi. There they met with a local clothmaker named Lydia. After they baptized Lydia and her household, she invited them to stay at her house. These were the first members of the church Paul wrote to in Philippians.

Paul was an influential leader. He traveled no matter what it cost him and wrote thirteen books of the Bible. He was busy for God.

"What then? Only that in every way, whether in pretense or in truth, Christ is proclaimed; and in this I rejoice. For I know that this shall turn

out for my deliverance through your prayers and the provision of the Spirit of Jesus Christ, according to my earnest expectation and hope, that I shall not be put to shame in anything, but that with all boldness, Christ shall even now, as always, be exalted in my body, whether by life or by death."

PHILIPPIANS 1:18-20

Paul spoke with his heart, and he was direct and honest. He preached "straight from the shoulder." There never was any attempt at flattery. Nevertheless, the truth was spoken in the spirit of tender affection and gentleness. Thus, with the warmth of inner conviction and deeply persuaded of the supreme importance of his message, the great missionary, dealing with each man as a father with his children, taught, exhorted, and encouraged.

I THESSALONIANS 1:1-5; 2:4, 5, 7-11

Paul is an iconic figure in history. Who else walked over ten thousand miles in a decade of their ministry; and who else had an endless desire to get the gospel to everyone?

But whatever things were gain to me, those things I have counted for loss for the sake of Christ. More than that, I count all things to be lost in view of the surpassing value of knowing Christ Jesus my Lord, for whom I have suffered the loss of all things, and count them but rubbish in order that I may gain Christ."

PHILIPPIANS 3:7-8

Material things were not what he was about. They were not his end goal. They were not lasting. In Philippians 4:11-12, he explains,

"Not that I speak from want; for I have learned to be content in whatever circumstances I am. I know how to get along with humble means, and I also know how to live in prosperity; in any and all circumstances I have learned the secret of being filled and going hungry, both of having abundance and suffering need."

Paul had many people along the way who opened their homes to him and shared with him and his companions. In Philippi he met Silas, Timothy, Luke, and Lydia. He was able to stay with Lydia's household. In Corinth, he stayed a year and a half, longer than anywhere else, with his dear friends Priscilla (Prisca) and Aquila. Aquila and Priscilla found their way to Corinth and settled there, pursuing their trade as tentmakers. When Paul, a tentmaker himself, came to Corinth, he went to see them, no doubt having heard of their faith in Christ. Paul lived and worked there with them while founding the Corinthian church. Priscilla and Aquila are described in the New Testament as providing a presence that strengthened the early church. Paul was generous in his recognition and acknowledgment of his indebtedness to them. They are mentioned six times in four different books of the New Testament, always named as a couple and never individually. Of those six references, Aquila's name is mentioned first only twice, and one of the times it was Paul's first encounter with them, probably meeting Aquila first.

Priscilla's name is mentioned first on four occasions, and this may indicate her equal status with her husband, or even possibly that Priscilla was thought of as the more prominent teacher and disciple.

"Greet Prisca and Aquila, my fellow workers in Christ Jesus, who for my life risked their own necks, to whom not only do I give thanks, but also all the churches of the Gentiles; also greet the church that is in their house."

ROMANS 16:3-5

"We give thanks to God, the Father of our Lord Jesus Christ, praying always for you, since we heard of your faith in Christ Jesus and the love which you have for all the saints; because of the hope laid up for you in heaven, of which you previously heard in the word of truth, the gospel, which has come to you, just as in all the world also it is constantly bearing fruit and increasing, even as it has been doing in you also since the day you heard of it and understood the grace of God in truth; just as you learned of it from Epaphras, our beloved fellow bond-servant, who is a faithful servant of Christ on our behalf, and he also informed us of your love in the Spirit."

COLOSSIANS 1:3-8

One can see Paul was thrilled to have a good report from this church he had been to in Colossae. Not that his letter to them doesn't have some concerns, but he is genuinely thankful they are still meeting and are showing others Christ's love. As Paul writes many of his letters from prison, one can see his love for those churches that have been planted. He is a great example of someone who loves fellow believers and desires for them to keep growing in their faith so they in turn may lead still more people to Christ.

Sometimes, I think we feel we do not measure up. We may ask, how can I lead others to Christ or how can I encourage them in their walk if I myself am so unworthy? But then, God gave us Paul. He was so full of himself, he persecuted Christians, and he thought he was more righteous than anyone. But God caused a miracle in his life and he became a new person. He knew that no matter how much he had sinned, God would change him, and he must tell everyone!

In the first eleven chapters of Romans, Paul tells us over and over that we are justified by faith, not by works. We may be a sinner, but God will work in our hearts. Then in 12:1-2, he tells us we are transformed.

"I urge you therefore, brethren, by the mercies of God, to present your bodies a living and holy sacrifice, acceptable to God, which is your spiritual service of worship. And do not be conformed to this world, but be transformed by the renewing of your mind, that you may prove what the will of God is, that which is good and acceptable and perfect."

God has given believers so much that Paul exhorts them to respond in grateful obedience. These were actually the first verses I ever memorized. I did not fully understand yet what being transformed actually meant. It is a process. Paul understood this, and he kept checking on the new churches he had started. But we can choose to grow and change. We must be determined. The following is a quote by Kay Arthur from a Precepts New Inductive Study Series Bible study I have been doing on Romans:

"Every day of my life I must remind myself that I am a child of God and have God, the Holy Spirit indwelling and empowering me to say no to sin and yes to God. Every day I must live in the truth that I can present the members of my body for righteousness because of this indwelling power of the Holy Spirit. Every day I must make it my will to live for God, I must choose to obey, to become more and more like Christ, to whom I have been joined. I must. I can. I will."

We were once sinners, but our faith set us free. Paul felt freed by being justified, and he was going to serve the one who set him free. Not only does he walk those ten thousand miles, but he then writes to those same churches from prison because he loves them. I have to say I have had that heart-pounding experience when I want to share the gospel with someone and am scared. But I also feel so excited after someone responds and comes to Christ. Maybe you will not be there to "catch the fruit" and see them come to Christ. But that is not the point. Since God tells us to love others more than ourselves, then wouldn't we want them to spend eternity in Heaven?

I am so thankful for the testimony of Paul and all the books he wrote that have given me hope in my walk through the years and have encouraged me to grow so that I can share my faith with someone else. Paul's journey is a strong reminder that each one of us can be used by God, no matter our background, and that we can tell others about Jesus and His saving grace.

"AND I SAID. 'WHO ART THOU. LORD?' AND THE LORD SAID. 'I AM JESUS WHOM YOU ARE PERSECUTING. BUT ARISE. AND STAND ON YOUR FEET: FOR THIS PURPOSE I HAVE APPEARED TO YOU. TO APPOINT YOU A MINISTER AND A WITNESS ... TO OPEN THEIR EYES SO THAT THEY MAY TURN FROM DARKNESS TO LIGHT... IN ORDER THAT THEY MAY RECEIVE FORGIVENESS OF SINS AND AN INHERITANCE AMONG THOSE WHO HAVE BEEN SANCTIFIED BY FAITH IN ME.'
ACTS 26: 15-18"

CHAPTER 30

Afterword

Living Our Life With Intention

Now that you've read these testimonies from other believers, you're probably energized and inspired to do more and live boldly. Ask yourself:

How are you bold for Christ?

How are you intentional in what you do?

How do you live a purposeful life?

These are rhetorical questions for you to ask yourself about your own journey.

As the testimonies started coming in, each one was SO different. Of course they would be, but I think in my limited initial vision, I thought they would say things differently. Some of the people chosen did not even mention the life events I thought would fit perfectly in my preliminary view of this project! BUT I always pray as I write each book that God would show me direction in what He wants in the book and give me discernment as to what to include. So as things moved along, I was excited to see it develop, not as I first envisioned, but into something more. I am hoping this enhances what you as a reader can gain from it. Instead of guiding the stories, I let God guide the contributors to tell their own story.

I was also flooded with scriptures. Every sermon or Bible study I heard or did seemed to relate somehow. I'd even shout out, "Hey, that ties in with my book!" I probably got an eye roll or two, but I got so excited. Our Bible and faith all ties together, so this was no surprise to me. I am sure there have been times when you thought the sermon on Sunday totally tied in with your own personal walk or Bible study that week. It solidifies what we learn in a special way.

And even though originally, this book was to only include testimonies, I am so glad I have also been able to share about some heroes of our faith who have passed on, but who were such great examples to us. And I have only shared a very few Bible characters who stood boldly for God. There are so many others!

Today, all around the world, Christians are being persecuted for their faith. They are making a stand and they feel that sense of urgency to share the Gospel of Jesus Christ so many will come to know the living God and live in eternity with Him.

Jesus tells the Samaritan woman in John chapter 4 verse 23,

> *"But an hour is coming, and now is, when the true*
> *worshipers shall worship the Father in spirit and truth;*
> *for such people the Father seeks to be His worshipers."*

My husband and I have worked in the Awana children's ministry for over thirty years. It is a worldwide organization for kids focusing on Bible memorization. Those who glibly say that children don't fully understand and are just learning by rote don't get the point. I have heard countless testimonies shared by older people who have said that they did not grow up in a Christian home, but their neighbor or grandma brought them to Awana, and later they remembered a verse that kept coming up in their mind, and it was instrumental in them accepting Christ. One of the verses that kept coming into my mind when I was considering this book is found in Romans 1:16,

> *"For I am not ashamed of the gospel, for it is the power of God for salvation to everyone who believes, to the Jew first and also to the Greek."*

This is a verse everyone in Awana memorized. Paul had been imprisoned and chased down by people, yet he wrote this. He would not let anything stop his boldness for Christ.

Paul wrote more books in the Bible than anyone else. He wanted everyone to know that you are righteous before God if you believe Jesus is the Son of God and died and rose again. It doesn't matter who you are, or what you have done in the past. It does not matter how you were raised. You see, Paul is the perfect person to share this because he previously had killed Christians, but he was now redeemed. In Romans 5:6-8, he writes,

> *"For while we were still helpless, at the right time Christ died for the ungodly. For one will hardly die for a righteous man; though perhaps for the good man someone would dare even to die. But God demonstrates His own love toward us, in that while we were yet sinners, Christ died for us."*

And lest you think you are not worthy, in 6:22-23, it says,

"But now having been freed from sin and enslaved to God, you derive your benefit, resulting in sanctification, and the outcome, eternal life. For the wages of sin is death, but the free gift of God is eternal life in Christ Jesus our Lord."

It does not get any plainer than that.

I have many people in my life I pray for daily who do not know Christ. It grieves my heart. I pray for boldness to share with others about eternity because it is going to become more difficult to do so. In 2 Timothy 4:2-4, Paul tells us to,

"Preach the word; be ready in season and out of season; reprove, rebuke, exhort, with great patience and instruction. For the time will come when they will not endure sound doctrine; but wanting to have their ears tickled they will accumulate for themselves teachers in accordance to their own desires; and will turn away their ears from the truth, and will turn aside to myths."

Working on this book helped me to take a closer look at my own faith walk, and other peoples' stories inspired me to be more purposeful in what I do each day. Oh dear one, read your Bible for yourself. Ask God to give you wisdom and open up to what it says. Share your faith like never before. Find ways to be **bold** and **intentional**.

"Radical obedience to Christ is not easy...It's not comfort, not health, not wealth, and not prosperity in this world. Radical obedience to Christ risks losing all these things. But in the end, such risk finds its reward in Christ. And he is more than enough for us."

David Platt, Radical:
Taking Back Your Faith from the American Dream

Are you ready to live BOLD?

To be bold is not just to live a normal everyday life, but it suggests instead a life that is "extra," a walk that is "more," and a mindset that is far more than ordinary.

Join our
LIVE BOLDLY GROUP
on Facebook and take
The 30 day challenge
*to **be more intentional,**
and live boldly!*

Study Questions

BOLD WHERE YOU ARE

1. Which person did you relate to the most and why? List 3 reasons.

_____

_____

_____

_____

_____

_____

_____

_____

_____

2. How did these examples display boldness? Choose 3 to discuss.

_____

_____

_____

_____

_____

_____

_____

_____

_____

_____

_____

_____

_____

_____

3. How can you be bold in your life at home? Sometimes we need to pray for ways to intentionally reach out. _____

_____

_____

_____

_____

_____

_____

_____

_____

_____

_____

_____

_____

_____

_____

_____

4. Think of 3 people or situations where you can intentionally reach out to minister to others. _____

_____

_____

_____

_____

_____

_____

_____

_____

_____

_____

_____

_____

_____

_____

BOLD AND BEYOND

1. Which person do you feel best represents boldness? Can you relate to

    this person?_____

    _____

    _____

    _____

    _____

    _____

    _____

    _____

    _____

    _____

    _____

    _____

    _____

    _____

    _____

    _____

    _____

2. These people gave there all for God. How do these characters display

    "sacrificial" boldness? _____

    _____

    _____

    _____

    _____

    _____

    _____

    _____

    _____

    _____

    _____

    _____

    _____

    _____

    _____

    _____

    _____

3. How does this inspire you to be more purposeful in your faith? Do you have a scripture passage that would reflect this type of faith?

_____

_____

_____

_____

_____

_____

_____

_____

_____

_____

_____

_____

_____

_____

4. Each of these people are great examples of living a life for God no matter the cost. Do you have a hero of faith you can share about?

_____

_____

_____

_____

_____

_____

_____

_____

_____

_____

_____

_____

_____

_____

_____

_____

BOLD IN THE BIBLE

1. Can you think of any other characters in the Bible you would consider bold that I have not listed? _____

_____

_____

_____

_____

_____

_____

_____

_____

_____

_____

_____

_____

_____

_____

2. What characteristics do each of these examples have that allow them

to be bold? _____

_____

_____

_____

_____

_____

_____

_____

_____

_____

_____

_____

_____

_____

_____

3. The Bible is full of examples of men and women who gave their all. Who has been the most influential to you?_____

_____

_____

_____

_____

_____

_____

_____

_____

_____

_____

_____

_____

_____

_____

_____

4. How has this book influenced you to live more boldly for the gospel? _____

_____

_____

_____

_____

_____

_____

_____

_____

_____

_____

_____

_____

_____

_____

5. What are ways you can start to purposefully go out of your comfort

zone?_____

_____

_____

_____

_____

_____

_____

_____

_____

_____

_____

_____

_____

_____

Colossians 3:12 Ministries

When I started writing books, I wasn't sure how far it would go. I just wanted to share Christ with as many people as possible and offer help and encouragement. Now, with three published books, Colossians 3:12 Ministries has been born.

It is a ministry to offer resources for people needing help figuring out how to best serve those around them. It offers resources for widows, addicts, single parents, and others.

Visit <u>www.col312ministries.com</u> for more info.

About The Author

Nicki Corinne White has a passion for studying and teaching God's Word. She has been leading Bible studies and discipling young women for many years. She is very involved in her local church with both the children's ministry and women's ministry. She has a tender heart for those who are hurting and those who are new to church. Nicki hopes to be an encouragement to those around her by lending a listening ear, kind word, or a biblical reminder. She also opens her home to share with others and serve others through hospitality on a regular basis, and believes we are all called to do this. Nicki feels blessed to have been able to use her story and personal experience to encourage others and hopes to expand this ministry through her writing.

Nicki is married to her husband, Craig. She has four children and currently has 6 grandchildren.

Nicki Corinne has previously published two books:

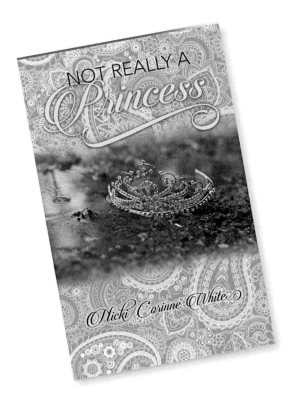

NOT REALLY A PRINCESS

Not Really A Princess is a redemption story dealing with grief, adoption, poverty, rejection and issues concerning widows. It begins in a small town in Washington where the author and her sister, Lisa were adopted at an early age. Through trying times they struggled both financially and emotionally. Their adoptive dad died when the author was 13 and they had no income. Moma sank into despair. Through this time Moma, Lisa and the author became believers in Christ as their Saviour. This gave them hope and an inner peace through years of being encouraged by others and studying God's Word. The final twenty-five years of Moma's life were her happiest times. She turned from bitterness created by adversity to a joyful life of praying for others. The author and her sister had their own changes and growth in their lives. She struggled with feelings of rejection, of truly believing others loved her and also accepting that her Moma was a truly renewed person. This story encompasses many genres and reaches out to those who need hope through difficult times. Hopefully it will be used as a tool by many to show others they can grow and change throughout their life. and It's Not About the Pie: A Fresh Look at Hospitality.

It's Not About the Pie:
A Fresh Look at Hospitality

It's Not About The Pie is a fresh look at hospitality. Author, Nicki Corinne White, often hears from people that they are not "gifted" in hospitality. It always makes her cringe a bit. She has always felt that, if there is a need we can meet, we should meet it. Her home is far from perfect, but she does not think that matters to most who enter her home. They are so thankful that they are welcome and look forward to their time whether it's for a dinner party, Bible study or just to share their heart. This book deals with how to be hospitable, ideas for decorating, recipes for tasting and how you can reach out to the needy. It focuses on what God wants our perspective to be on inviting others into our home, why we should have others into our home, and the fact that your home does not have to be perfect. Just open. It will also give you encouragement about how to reach out to widows, orphans and others in need. The key is to be willing and work at ways to keep your home open. Maybe this book's purpose is to show you ideas that will allow you to make a few things, so you will feel more comfortable having someone stay with you.

It's Not About The Pie also gives examples of people helping people in a variety of ways. From an older woman befriending a newcomer in town to a church paying expenses for someone who has cancer and cannot pay the bills to the neighbor watching little children, so someone can go out for a long needed date night. It also shares Bible verses on what our role truly is that God has shown us in His Word.

t's Not About The Pie will inspire readers to have the encouragement they need to welcome the neighbor that they have been wanting to know, the young widow with little kids who just needs a fun night or someone going through chemo whose spouse is beside himself not knowing what to do and just in need of a listening ear. Maybe someone has a guest room that is only used once a year but could be used to help a missionary family or a college student who has nowhere to go during spring break. There are needs everywhere for us to meet. This book will inspire our hearts to go beyond the norm.

Contact Us

Nicki Corinne White is available for book signings and speaking engagements. To get in touch with her team, please email us or message us through her website.

nickicorinnewhite@gmail.com

www.nickicorinne.com

facebook

instagram

pinterest